To James —

In honor of our
mutual interest in
networks.

Jeffrey Stamps

Jessica Lipnack

Sept. 24, 1996

THE
AGE OF THE
NETWORK

Other Books by Jessica Lipnack & Jeffrey Stamps

The TeamNet Factor: Bringing the Power of Boundary Crossing Into
the Heart of Your Business

The Networking Book: People Connecting with People

Networking: The First Report and Directory

Holonomy: A Human Systems Theory (*by Jeffrey Stamps*)

THE
AGE OF THE
NETWORK

Organizing Principles for the 21st Century

JESSICA LIPNACK
AND JEFFREY STAMPS

John Wiley & Sons, Inc.

New York · Chichester · Brisbane · Toronto · Singapore

To

Miranda Shoket Stamps and Eliza Lipnack Stamps
our children who are the future

•

Kate and Ben Taylor
dear friends of our generation

•

Bucky and Anne Fuller
and our parents and grandparents

ACKNOWLEDGMENTS

Jim Childs is the smart, unassuming, persistent person responsible for getting this book into print. From the time we finished *The TeamNet Factor*, our last book, Jim called monthly, asking, always gently, for the next book. Authors dream of such persistence from publishers. Jim also contributed much thought to this book, including the inspiration for future trends. And, once again, he read and made suggestions on every chapter. Jim, thank you for your generosity and easy way of working.

Thanks to Mike Snell for introducing us to Jim and to Darryl Landvater, president of Oliver Wight Publications, an inspiring businessman and generous counselor, who hired Jim.

Next, thanks to Debra Church-Smith, our long-time colleague at The Networking Institute. Seven years already, Deb, of spirit lifting, opportunity spotting, client supporting, workshop making, mega-communicating, and book writing, not to mention a couple of children. There should be 100 words for thank you here.

Thanks for the title of this book go to George Gendron, editor of *Inc.* magazine. George ran an excerpt from *The TeamNet Factor* in his monthly "FYI" column, titling it "The Age of the Network." We saw it and realized that we had the title for this book. A few months later, we were sitting in our local coffee shop, talking with Bob Elmore, head of Business Systems Consulting at Arthur Andersen & Co., when he leaned forward and said, "What you're talking about are 'organizing principles for the 21st century.'" Bingo, the subtitle.

Deep bows to six people dedicated enough to line-edit the entire manuscript without being asked: Kathi Albertini (for responsiveness and critical advice), Lilly Evans ("Most Prompt Reader" award), Judy Laws, David Stephenson, Joan Vitello, and Marion Metcalf. Marion was also "guardian angel" for this book, always asking how it was going, sending encouraging words with a steadfast consistency that was very calming. Al Gilman ably assisted Marion in this noble effort. Thanks, you two.

Another group scrutinized parts of the manuscript and offered critical comments: Frank Alla (an expert on trust), Harry Brown, Martin Gillo, Thommy Haglund, Bob Joines, Nancy Ledford, Mike Plummer, Günther Singer, Bill Smith, Frank Starmer, and Joe Szocik.

When Elizabeth Meyer Lorentz, our long-time mentor on the coordinator role in networks, learned that we were writing this book, she wrote a detailed background paper, which we drew on extensively for chapter 7. Elizabeth, again and forever, our dear friend.

Mark Abramson, Rebecca Adamson, Karen Belding, Forrest Bjerkaas, David Brace, Don Brown, Andy Campbell, Allan Cohen, Camen Criswell, Dennis Egan, Manny Elkind, Paul Fogleman, Susan Goran, Rogier Gregoire, Damon Hemmerdinger, Mallika Henry, Karl Leatham, Peter+Trudy Johnson-Lenz, Gregg Lichtenstein, Geri Lincoln, Judy Lucarelli, Gösta Lundqvist, Annie Marascia, Oliver Markley, Bill Miller, Eddie Molloy, Lyn Montague, Charlene O'Brien (and family), Doug Parker, Frank Reece, Will Roberts, Debra Amidon Rogers, David Ryder, Karim Saouli, Charles Savage, Ann Schwartz, Judith Gilman Schwenk, Navjeet Singh, Gail Snowden, Nova Spivack, Evelyne Steward, Peter Thibeault, Nancy Weeks, Lavinia Weissman, David Williams, and Duncan Work all contributed ideas.

Special thanks to our "TeamNet Workshoppers" for participating in our ongoing discussions of trust and social capital.

Sting provided *Fields of Gold*, the background music. Tom Peters, great networker, gave *The TeamNet Factor* its first name-recognition boost. The Internet greased the lines of communication, joining in "the pod." J. Gordon Lippincott, founder of Lippincott and Margulies, the New York design firm, sent us the logo that appears on the front of this book. We've used it as our corporate mark since 1983, when we received it. Thanks, again, Gordon.

Sandy Billings, Rita and Bill Cleary, and Anne Starr, all of The Learning Circle, spread the word. Rick Berenson and David Cray kept the business going at critical moments. Ann Stamps instantly responded to a crisis. Eric Lipnack and Carol Roman eased a painful transition. Erwin and Marianne Jaffe and Judy Smith were always there with love. Bill and Pam Johnson's early sponsorship was a powerful launching pad, with great help from Ulf Fagerquist. Virginia Hine and Bucky Fuller continue to inspire.

Our two teenagers may have sometimes gone without dinner while we wrote this book, but they thrived. Miranda Stamps attained a rare (even for adults) level of maturity in 1994, studying, working, speaking, being with friends, and, most important, driving. Eliza Stamps learned to counsel, bike, traverse the city (and the world), do art, and study, all with originality. You were a toddler, Mirmy, when we started this networking work, and Liza, you were just a pregnancy. Now you are vibrant networkers yourselves and our closest advisors. Girls, we thank you and we love you.

Jessica Lipnack and Jeffrey Stamps
West Newton, Massachusetts
July 1994

CONTENTS

LIST OF
ILLUSTRATIONS

INTRODUCTION
THE NETWORK COMES OF AGE

The network is coming of age as a mature, useful, and pervasive form of organization. Networks have been around for a long time, but now they are moving from the informal to the formal, from dealing with peripheral concerns to doing "real work"—getting things done and coping with complexity.

Life has become too complicated for hierarchy and bureaucracy. With change as the underlying driver, organizations need more speed and flexibility, greater scope and sharper intelligence, more creativity and shared responsibility. Teams offer part of the answer—our collective rediscovery of ancient human knowledge about the power of small groups. Networks—of teams and other groups joined together, which we call "teamnets"—offer another, newer part of the answer. The rest of the answer to our organizational challenge lies in the accumulated wisdom of hierarchy and bureaucracy, their timeless elements.

Huh? The wisdom of hierarchy? The timelessness of bureaucracy? We feel a little like Nixon going to China for this message:

Don't throw out your hierarchy. Save some bureaucracy.

We have been known as the "networking people" since we wrote *Networking: The First Report and Directory*, our first book, published in 1982, the year we founded The Networking Institute. Networks have been our mission, our passion, and our bread and butter.

This book puts networks in the context of earlier forms of organization, offering a way to use the new powers of networks together with the best mix of hierarchy, bureaucracy, and small groups.

When we finished the manuscript for *The TeamNet Factor* at the end of 1992, we felt strangely unfinished. That book made the case for networks with numerous examples, general principles, practical tools, and exciting possibilities. We still needed to place networks, the emergent form of organization, in a broader and deeper context.

The Age of the Network is the "prequel" to *The TeamNet Factor.*

Read *The Age of the Network* first. It is shorter, has a broader focus, and is more personal, exploring the underpinnings of networks, the links among people, their relationships, and consuming issue of trust. Here, using new examples, we offer an executive summary of the core principles and practices that are expansively detailed in *The TeamNet Factor.*

The two books are complementary. Each stands alone, with unique elements and focus, yet they share a conceptual coherence, spectrum of examples, and writing style. We offer some pointers to the companion text as well as to other chapters in this one, our restrained effort to emulate electronic random access hypertext in a serial printed book.

The Industrial Age medium of our Information Age message captures again the tricky transitional reality of this millennium-approaching time that we inhabit. The forces of old and new seem equally demanding, and the zigzags of life, both personally and globally, seem more extreme and more frequent with each passing year.

This book will help you cope with change, forge your own destiny, and join with others to accomplish together what you cannot do alone.

The Age of the Network has five sections:

I. "Looking From Above," the introductory overview (chapter 1);
II. "The Big Idea": how all the forms of organization fit together and why this moment is so timely for networking (chapters 2 and 3);
III. "Principles and Practice": tools for networks and how to use them (chapters 4, 5, and 6);
IV. "Expanding Links": looking in more depth at the network's most distinguishing features (chapters 7 and 8); and
V. "Looking Ahead" with trends for the future (chapter 9).

We all have personal learning preferences, that is, what we need to feel comfortable with new ideas and information. In both books, we bring out concepts with a rich variety of examples and offer methodology along with vision. This gives you an opportunity to see networks through multiple lenses, since no one view is complete.

- Short for time or want to get the whole context before a sequential reading? Skim the book by paging through and reading the heads and indented text to get the basic ideas. Check out the graphics and bulleted lists if you have a few more minutes.
- Some people tell us that they start with the first and last chapters of books, hence our overview in "Looking From Above" and conclusions in "Looking Ahead."
- Just want the big ideas? Read the first three chapters.
- Is practical application your first test? Go for the three chapters in Section III.
- Looking for what's really new here, the human dimension, and trends? Read the three chapters in Sections IV and V.

Enhance your understanding by comparing examples from your own life with our principles and observations. Think about your most successful team experience; then use your imagination to visualize what's possible.

Most important, remember that the Age of the Network belongs to all of us. The future of our organizations—our organic ways of being and doing together—rests in our collective hands.

SECTION I

LOOKING FROM ABOVE

CHAPTER 1

WHY NETWORKS? THE 30,000-FOOT VIEW

A global revolution is underway, a social upheaval in organization that involves you and everyone you know. It shakes every place of work, quakes the foundations of our biggest institutions and our smallest groups, even sends quivers into our homes and communities. It swirls through organizations of all sizes, in all sectors, in all countries. Regardless of gender, race, creed, or economic status, people are turning their organizations upside down, on their sides, and inside out.

> *The network is emerging as the signature form of organization in the Information Age, just as bureaucracy stamped the Industrial Age, hierarchy controlled the Agricultural Era, and the small group roamed in the Nomadic Era.*

Does this mean "smash the boundaries," "tear down the hierarchy," and "dismantle the bureaucracy"?

"Clear out the old to make way for the new" goes the conventional wisdom. Appealing as these slogans of management revolution might be, they are misleading. Has any organization you know rid itself entirely of hierarchy and bureaucracy? What is more important, should it?

To develop healthy, flexible, intelligent organizations for the 21st century, we need to harvest the best of the past and combine it with what is really new. Surely, some learning from thousands of years of organizational life must be worth keeping. There must be continuity as well as change.

So, what is timeless in hierarchy and precious in bureaucracy? Where's the "baby" and what's the "bath water"? What should we throw out, what is best to keep, and what is both new and enduring?

Every day, our interaction with traditional organizations presents us with the personal challenge of learning how to function in groups—small and large. Couples argue about how to organize the housework; coworkers squabble about who's in charge; politicians debate how to balance their power, even to the point of "reinventing government." New ways of doing things are growing in, between, and alongside "the way things are and always have been."

Each of us participates in many small groups. Every encounter, every meeting, every moment spent planning the future is an opportunity to do a little organizational design. With each new set of connections, we realize anew how connected things really are—among people, small groups, companies, cities, nations, and every other human grouping.

Millions of people are active participants in the organizational revolution propelling world civilization into the Age of the Network. The creation of this next age belongs to all of us as we design the organization of the future, which looks as different from the one of the past as the railroad boxcar does from the computer chip.

RIDING THE TRANSITIONAL WAVE

We don't arrive in the next century without a heritage. Today's generations straddle two eras, the graying industrial one behind and the sleek
information one ahead. Just a decade ago, this was Sunday supplement speculation; today, it is a mainstream idea.

Collectively, we are in the middle of the transition. Too far in to go
back, yet not far enough along to see how it's going to turn out, we are
actors in the drama, playing out the awesome zigzags of truly changing times.

Today, in transition, we naturally live with all types of organization.

- Hierarchy, the top-down pyramid, has been pronounced dead, yet
  lives and, in most circumstances, still holds final rule.
- Even as virtually everyone vigorously complains about it and
  finds ways to skirt it, bureaucracy, with its neatly stacked, specialized boxes, continues to spew out more policies and procedures,
  rules and regulations.
- Small groups and teams are in—from the shop floor and front
  desk to the executive suite and boardroom.
- At the same time, new *networks* are forming, both within and
  among older organizational forms.

How do these forms fit together to create the most effective organization for a variety of circumstances, including your specific situation? To help answer this question, we need to start with a broad view.

FROM THE 19TH TO THE 21ST CENTURY

At 30,000 feet, the world looks considerably different from the way it
does on the ground. The best leaders sometimes see their organizations from such a distance. From a great height, what do you really see
in the mind's eye? An organization chart? Images of spreadsheets and

charts of accounts? Sensations of the politics of a board meeting? The faces of customers?

If you're like Bob Barry, a line of business partner-in-charge at KPMG Peat Marwick and a member of its international executive board, you know the old filters of traditional structures don't work today. "For us to be successful, we can't work in the little boxes anymore," says Barry, one of thousands of executives running a 21st-century organizational "car" with a 19th-century chassis.

Peat Marwick is nearly 100 years old. It was literally born in the Industrial Age in 1897. For decades, it was *the* premiere accounting firm, serving the captains of Western industry—until it hit the 1970s. Suddenly, the venerable business took an unpredictably sharp turn into dimensions that it never imagined. It had to cope with the impact of information technology, like the perplexing fact that many of its clients highly value information that KPMG should—but could not— provide. And it faced a global economy where the sun never sets and competition never ceases.

In the late 1980s, it also suffered merger mania (which is how the "KPMG" got in front of "Peat Marwick") and it acquired a number of American firms. Merging fits the industrial dictum that bigger is better, a truism under challenge. But the underlying nature of professional services, with partners and offices everywhere serving geographically distributed customers, has led Peat tentatively toward redesigning itself as an Information Age organization.

By 1993, the sprawling firm had decided to restructure completely, moving from geographic units to lines of business—from physical to conceptual boundaries.

Barry, who heads part of the new financial services organization, says, "I've got to think financial services. But we've always thought geography. It's hard for people to think across boundaries."

Barry knows that the 19th-century bureaucracy has to make room for the 21st-century network, which means that he also has to consider the role of technology.

When we think about the future, it is nearly always in terms of technology—the emissionless car, the voice-activated computer, the solar-powered community. "But the technological innovations influence, cause, and precipitate organizational changes," says Kathleen Barry Albertini, a technology expert working on economic development issues.[1] Just as generations of new technology blur in year-end retrospectives, our organizations are changing faster than the mind's eye can see.

THE CIA NEEDS A NEW MISSION

How can we solve the problems of the 21st century with 19th-century organizations? Tomorrow's company is as different from its 19th-century ancestor as a steam engine is from a database engine.

Two hundred years is a very long life span for an organization. Most companies don't make it past 40. (If a dog year is seven human years, then an "org" year is two.) Regardless of how long they have survived so far, most mature companies have trembled through an organizational earthquake in the past few decades that has left them dizzy.

If times are tough on Peat Marwick, just think about what America's Central Intelligence Agency (CIA) is going through. Until the late 1980s, the CIA had everything under control, so to speak. It had relatively stable competition and a steady cash flow, an enviable position for any organization. Then a completely unexpected thing happened. In 1989, the walls came down, and its traditional market—in fact, its whole *raison d'être*—evaporated overnight. The European structures of Marx and Lenin, icons of the Industrial Age, disappeared, depositing one-tenth of humanity in the postcommunist era at once.[2]

The whole game of spying is unlike its pre-Age of the Network self. "We are now aware of the existence of many highly organized, sophisticated networks of corruption operating on an industrial scale," said one *oil company* in *The Wall Street Journal*. The lead story on January 6, 1994, says that "global spy networks eavesdrop on projects of petroleum firms," aided by technology in a high-stakes game in which information is the currency.[3]

Spies are hardly the only problem for the oil companies, which, once flush with cash, now anxiously await the next lurch in prices. Rushed to change like the CIA and in the same fix as KPMG Peat Marwick, they have many unlikely companions in the Age of the Network:

- Hyatt Hotels, Qantas Airways, Air Canada, and the rest of the increasingly fluid travel and hospitality industry.
- Advanced Micro Devices, IBM, Motorola, and every other high-tech company propelled by increasing power and decreasing costs.
- *The Boston Globe, The Washington Post*, the Dow Jones/Ottaway Newspaper Group, and other publishers, which worry as much about systems integration and their role in the digital future as they do about the news.
- Kellogg's, Giant Foods, and the rest of the food industry, in which "perishable" has taken on a whole new meaning with global markets and just-in-time distribution.
- The Catawba Valley Hosiery Association (some 200 North Carolina firms that produce half of the hosiery in the United States), Furniture/New York (40 small furniture designers and manufacturers working together to increase exports), Appalachia's ACENET (dozens of small manufacturers joined in networks to serve new markets), and other small firms that need a critical mass to be players on the global economic stage.

The need to network certainly is hitting health care. Consider how it looks to the 78,000 people who belong to the American Association of Critical Care Nurses, whose president, Joan Vitello, says, "Patients and their families require a seamless network of care," demanding a very different approach from the superspecialized contemporary world of medicine.

Teams and networks of care, yes, but also elsewhere in the health industry: among consumers in insurance pools and alliances; among doctors in physician networks; among hospitals to share high-cost equipment and facilities; and among all these players and more in health maintenance organizations.

THE NETWORK AGE HOSPITALITY COMPANY

Darryl Hartley-Leonard, president of Hyatt Hotels Corporation in Chicago, had just returned from a 1993 luncheon meeting at the White House, where 12 company heads from widely divergent industries had come together to discuss national trade policy with the president. "Hyatt cannot solve America's international trade problem alone," Hartley-Leonard told us, "and neither can any other single company."

Likewise, Hyatt Hotel Corporation depends on relationships. A management company with 55,000 employees, it has 104 primary customers, each a separately owned hotel. Hyatt doesn't own its hotels; it manages, and most of what it manages is change, discrepancies in the routine. At any moment, 10 percent of the hotels are having some sort of crisis that requires emergency attention: the Persian Gulf War disrupts travel to Hawaii, a general manager suddenly resigns, Marriott springs a promotion.

Like KPMG Peat Marwick, Hyatt is a natural network—in this case a network of just over 100 hotels.

Without its relationships with customers, the people who show up to register at the hotels and use their facilities, Hyatt has no business. Hyatt works with travel agents, tour companies, conference planners, and others who control portions of the overall market to reach customers.

Then there are the suppliers. Hyatt liked Ely's Cheesecake, the product of a small Chicago bakery, so much that its own chefs decided to buy directly from them, "outsourcing" it. This is a mission-critical supplier to Hyatt. What is the dessert menu without cheesecake?

Multiple, complex relationships enmesh Hyatt Hotels with a variety of other companies. Taken as a whole, it's a $2 billion company;

taken apart, it is not a business. This is a very different industry than it was even 20 years ago, when companies could go it alone and the future seemed reasonably predictable.

TAKING THE CEO VIEWPOINT

To see the whole of organizations today, we have to move to the 30,000-foot view. We can see large patterns—interconnecting highways, metropolises, hinterlands, and natural geographic areas from that height. Organizationally, we see groups that spread across cities and continents, making partners of suppliers and customers; informationally, we see data and communication pulsing through new arteries of connection.

Even two generations ago, we couldn't easily envision the world from this perspective. We didn't have the ordinary, everyday mental model of the earth as a whole, so conspicuously visible in pictures taken from space.

The globe as a whole is personal in many ways—through media like television, telephones, faxes, and the Internet (the global computer network accessible by a local phone call); and through markets, cultural styles, environmental changes, and other relationships of world scope. The challenge for every one of us is to develop individually yet join with others near and far, locally and globally. To be, in short, both "we" and "me," a part of the whole.

The whole–part challenge applies to organizations as well as people. A company is a whole made up of organizational components, such as divisions, departments, and groups, and is a part of larger wholes, such as alliances, industries, and markets.

Imagine sitting on the edge of a company, where the CEO does, taking that whole–part view.

Naturally taking a big-picture view of the world, CEOs of tiny enterprises and giants straddle the corporate boundary. They look both ways at once, being simultaneously inside and outside.

Not long ago, only a few people needed to take the inside–outside CEO view. In the smartest Network Age organizations, everyone learns to think like a CEO. Everyone can make the best decisions from this vantage point. "I ask the leadership team to wear two hats," says AT&T's CEO, Robert Allen. "I say, 'Come to our management meetings and represent your businesses.' But there are times when I ask you to put on *my* hat on behalf of the shareholders and help me make decisions that cross business-unit boundaries."[4]

Even CEOs must expand their views; simply looking in and out is insufficient for navigating through complexity. Knowing the business is no longer enough. Now CEOs must understand everything from the global economy and the politics of Eastern Europe to the effect of newborns on knowledge worker productivity and the cost of grief if one of them dies.

Success in the 21st century requires both *global* knowledge and *local* knowledge, understanding the "big picture" and the specific details. It also requires people to be both competitive and cooperative, simultaneously self-assertive individually and interdependently joined with others.

All the key pieces of the puzzle—from strategy to operations, from mission to service, from customers to shareholders, from competitors to partners—are part of the mental model of the person taking the CEO's view in the Age of the Network. The next question is how to frame those pieces. What is the overall design of your organization?

FOUR AGES OF ORGANIZATION

Mentally draw the big picture of your organization. Do you see levels of hierarchy connecting specialized boxes of bureaucracy? Is control top-down and are the boxes mutually exclusive? Do you belong in one and only one box?

TRADITIONAL ORGANIZATION

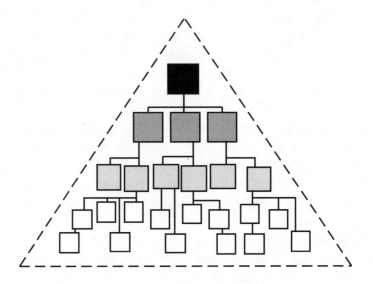

If so, you are working in a 19th-century organization, an Industrial Age machine. This is not good news if your world is turning upside down around you with speed-of-light communication.

Even if the box-chart pyramid is a cliché, it is still the only mental model for most of business and the public sector. It reflects organizational learning gathered over three great eras.

- First was the age of the camp fire, when nomadic small groups hunted and gathered.
- Then agriculture sprang up, and with it hierarchy, the top-down organizations still with us 12,000 years later.

- Next, with industry, came the steam engine bureaucracies, spread out across departments, divisions, and subsidiaries.

Today, everyone knows the traditional pyramid is out of synch with how work gets done and how decisions are made. For more than one company or agency, the conventional organization chart is a map to the obstructions to getting work done, the mountains to climb, and the rivers to ford.

We are many decades into the fourth era, driven by information, the *Age of the Network*.

- Now we have networks, groups of people working across boundaries of all kinds as knowledge replaces resources as the new source of wealth.

FROM BOXES TO PEPPERONI

How would you like a pizza instead of a pyramid?[5]

"Our organization chart . . . looks like a pizza with a lot of pepperoni sitting on it," Eastman Chemical Company's Chairman and CEO, Earnest W. Deavenport, Jr., tells *Business Week*.[6] "We did it in circular form to show that everyone is equal in the organization. No one dominates the other. The white space inside the circles is more important than the lines." The "white space?" Look below the surface and "see" the domain in which people collaborate.

Eastman provides an excellent, concrete example of an organization that combines teams, hierarchy, bureaucracy, and networks (see chapter 3, "Turning Hierarchy on its Side"). Among the management practices of this $4 billion spinoff from Eastman Kodak Company is a startling one. The company has replaced some key senior executive functions in mission-critical areas with "self-directed work teams." Five people manage manufacturing, for instance, as a team in which leaders rotate every quarter.

Shared leadership is one characteristic of organizations arising in the Age of the Network. Networks are meeting the challenge of

EASTMAN CHEMICAL COMPANY'S PIZZA CHART

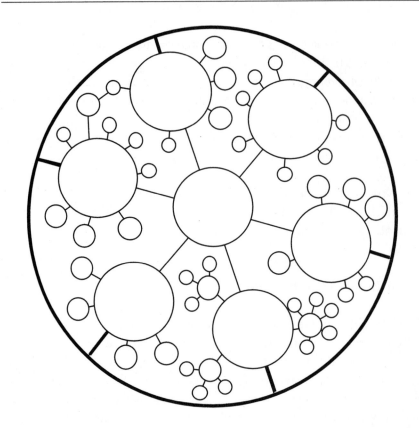

adapting to a new reality of time in a small world where the sun is always rising and never setting, changing forever the human experience of the fourth dimension.

EXPANDING IN A NEW DIMENSION

In the Industrial Age, we conquered space as the search for new worlds took us to the landing on the moon. By combining the great might of our machines with our imaginations, we pushed back the limits of terrestrial space. Now there is no place else to go on earth because everyone is a neighbor.

We are now global. The frontiers of our local
space have closed. Time is the new frontier.

With electronic technology widespread, anyone can talk to anyone and some can talk to everyone—by voice, by computer, by video. Place no longer means that you can be in only one of them; mutually exclusive locations have become relics of the past. Work rolls continuously around the world, following the sun, yet is instantly accessible all the time by everyone whenever they need it. Boundaries are conceptual, not physical, in virtual workplaces and need to be completely reconceived so that "physical site" thinking is no longer a limitation.

The electronic, speed-of-light Information Age
redefines ordinary, human-scale space and time.

A global economy and workplace are not just revolutionizing bigness. They affect us all and are accessible to any of us, whether as a teen on the Internet, a small furniture company in an export network, or a global CEO who lives on a plane.

"Change," which Tom Peters considers a pathetic word to stand for the uproarious revolution upon us,[7] is constant. "Crazy times call for crazy organizations," he says. In the Age of the Network, living in the =fourth dimension can be intense. More people are coping with more change than ever before. Are you? Time, as in a lifetime, has dramatically accelerated.

Once, a job lasted for a lifetime. Now the average person will change careers five times. Tomorrow, you will measure the half-life of a job in months, weeks, and days, as long as it takes to get another one. You will move from project to project, each one requiring your full concentration even while you have other things on your mind. The person you fought with mercilessly in your last job may be your boss in your new one—or your customer, or even your partner. Such is life today in Silicon Valley and many other places around the globe.

Most organizations are operating in the Age of the Network, whether they know it, like it, or want it. One obvious indicator is the proliferation of connections with other organizations. They take many names—"strategic alliances," "joint ventures," "outsourcing partnerships," and "flexible business networks," to name a few—linking customers, suppliers, and competitors. When executive, staff, and line colleagues form multiple, overlapping teams, they too are exploding in numberless cross-functional projects, horizontal corporations, and virtual enterprises.

Some companies—some organizations of every type—are already living in a flexible, richly connected, high-trust, high-performance, 21st-century design. They have agility and speed. They're competitive, *and* they retain heart.

• *They cross, but do not smash, boundaries.*

In networks, people work closely with clients, customers, vendors, suppliers, and even competitors. They know how to maintain boundaries without being immobilized by them, how to hold joint allegiances, how to balance conflicting interests, and how to tap resources beyond their own four walls, creating situations where everyone wins. Boundaries are the basis for self-identity and diversity, and even the Big 3 auto makers are crossing them. Together, they have a dozen consortia underway, investigating everything from the electric car to better crash dummies.[8]

• *They manage co-opetition.*

Networks allow you to cooperate and compete at the same time. Without both competition and cooperation, you cannot succeed in turbulent times that require flexibility, nimbleness, and learning, regardless of the size of your enterprise. "Co-opetition" puts these two apparent opposites into a dynamic dance.

• *They work in teamnets—networks of teams.*

To work across boundaries, people form local teams that bridge time and distance in networks. A team from Massachusetts General Hospital works with its counterpart at Brigham and Women's Hospital as Boston's two health care giants work through the details of their merger. Little teams make up big networks.

ORGANIZING PRINCIPLES PUT INTO PRACTICE

What are the "Organizing Principles for the 21st Century," and how can you make use of them?

Some common patterns underlie all networks that are eminently applicable in many arenas. When a community of practitioners applies the principles, they improve them through experiment and experience. You can check our patterns against your own experience.

CONCEPTUAL TOOLS FOR NETWORKS

Networks—the organizations once considered fringe phenomena—now are moving to center stage.

We have focused on networks and networking for 15 years, gathering information and insights, developing theory, testing it through practice, and writing about it—which provoked more information, theory, practice, and writing. We see five key organizing principles for the 21st century:

- *Unifying Purpose*
  Purpose is the glue and the driver. *Common views, values, and goals hold a network together. A shared focus on desired results keeps a network in synch and on track.*
- *Independent Members*
  Independence is a prerequisite for interdependence. *Each member of the network, whether a person, company, or country, can stand on its own while benefiting from being part of the whole.*
- *Voluntary Links*
  Just add links. *The distinguishing feature of networks is their links, far more profuse and omnidirectional than in other types of organization. As communication pathways increase, people and groups interact more often. As more relationships develop, trust strengthens, which reduces the cost of doing business and generates greater opportunities.*
- *Multiple Leaders*
  Fewer bosses, more leaders. *Networks are leaderful, not leaderless. Each person or group in a network has something unique to contribute at some point in the process. With more than one leader, the network as a whole has great resilience.*
- *Integrated Levels*
  Networks are multilevel, not flat. *Lumpy with small groups and clustered with coalitions, networks involve both the hierarchy and the "lower-archy," which leads them to action rather than simply to making recommendations to others.*

Big businesses like Eastman Chemical Company and small ones like Harry Brown's EBC Industries, local fire departments and the networks springing up among the agencies of the federal government, communities on the Internet, and companywide initiatives to accelerate learning all reflect these principles (see chapter 4, "A Pocket Tool for Teamnets"). They show up within organizations, as cross-functional teams and self-directed groups, and they structure relations among organizations, like strategic alliances and flexible business networks.

BELIEVE IN THE CREDO "THOSE WHO DO, PLAN"

A geographically distributed, functionally divided, or multitime zone, cross-boundary group needs to involve everyone it touches as much as possible to succeed. A plan created by one group and handed to another doesn't work in a network. Thus the dictum "Those Who Do, Plan." *People charged with doing work need to plan it for themselves.*

The best networks take the time necessary to clarify their purpose to the point where they can articulate it as a work plan. The people who will carry them out do the best plans, whether formal or informal, the ones that work and remain flexible. Even the plans themselves are not the point. It's the participatory *planning* that brings people into synch to accomplish things together across boundaries.

Networks are an organic form of organization, which means you need to understand them as a process as well as a structure. New networks start small and grow through phases:

- an initial, sometimes long startup phase;
- an intense, sometimes short launch phase;
- an often exciting performance phase;
- a frequently surprising test phase; and, finally,
- a completion phase.

At each stage of development, the five principles presented earlier offer a different utility. In chapter 5, "Rx for Monday Morning," we show how to use these principles for assessing organizational opportunities at startup and as a planning agenda for launch.

MATCH THE WORK WITH THE RIGHT ORGANIZATION

Networks are proliferating, but that doesn't mean they are always the best way to organize.

> *You can match the work to the right form of organization by understanding what teams can do, when hierarchy applies, what is useful in bureaucracy, what circumstances call for networks—and how to fit them all together.*

Size and scope, the pace of change, and the core technology driving the business are all considerations. (Chapter 6 "The Hinge of History," offers a "how-to" at the strategic level.)

- Is your scope local or global or both? How big should the group be? How can you retain the benefits of being small as you grow larger?
- While we all face an increased pace of change, the velocity is not the same everywhere. Environment strongly influences the nature of organizations, forcing more organic development in fast-changing surroundings and allowing more mechanical approaches where the pace is slower.
- Technology, particularly information technology, also influences organizational architecture. In the Age of the Network, connective technologies complement connective organizations. It is much easier for a networked organization to gain an organizational advantage from networked technology than for hierarchy-bureaucracy to do so.

THE DIFFERENCE OF EXPANDING LINKS

Links—the connective tissue extending in every direction and joining people across organizations, distance, and time—are at the heart of the Age of the Network. Whereas once a person knew perhaps a few hundred others, today his or her Rolodex may contain 10,000 names. Above all, abundant links in every direction make the network different from the organizations that came before—bureaucracies with their horizontal hand-offs from department to department, hierarchies with their top-down commands, and small groups with their one-to-one relationships. In a network, you connect up, down, out, and around.

The links of the network climb the chains of command like ivy and wrap all the way around the globe. Because the network enhances access to others rather than impedes it, even more people come into connection with one another, crossing organizations, anytime and anywhere.

COME IN, MADRAS, INDIA

Frank Starmer's "laboratory without walls" is an example of a connected organization. We met Frank—well, we've never met Frank in person, though we communicate with him frequently. Our introduction was unusual.

The phone rang one day. It was Rainer Hochkoeppler calling from Basel, Switzerland. He had read our books on networks and was inquiring about us coming to Zurich to do a workshop on our latest, *The TeamNet Factor*. Although he was familiar with us, we had never heard of him before, which he realized. As a reference, he followed our first phone call with a fax, recommending that we contact "My best American networking friend, Professor Frank Starmer, at Duke University."

So we called Professor Starmer to learn more. "He's in India until May," we were told. "Do you have access to the Internet? You can send him a message at frank@rodney.mc.duke.edu."

"Really?" we asked, incredulous. Yes, we had access to the Internet, but with India? Though a leader in software development, India also is famous for its erratic telephone system, on which the Internet depends. Never mind the general communication problems that plague the country: it takes months for letters to arrive, and people can't even send money abroad to buy books.

"He'll get it," we were assured.

That night we skeptically fired off a message to Professor Starmer, explaining who we were and hoping for the best.

By the next morning, we'd received the first of many detailed messages from Madras, India, where Frank, a professor of cardiology and computer sciences and trained as an electrical and biomedical engineer, as well as an early electronic networking pioneer, was spending a year, continuing in his ongoing role as coordinator of a global network of scientists doing basic research on excitable cells. (He also confirmed that our skepticism about the Internet was valid. "Indian e-mail is not really very reliable," he said. "We have a rather up-and-down link between here and our gateway in Bombay, and particularly during the monsoon season, just finished, all bets are off as to when e-mail arrives.")

We asked Frank who was in his "Excitable Cells Lab Without Walls," and he sent back an e-mail message with the names and electronic addresses of 32 people circling the globe. It includes scientists in his home lab at Duke, as well as:

Max Planck Institute in Heidelberg, Germany • University of Chicago • University of Pittsburgh • Syracuse University • Montreal Heart Center • Boston University • University of North Carolina • Moscow's Cardiac Center • University Santiago de Compostelo • University of Freiburg • University of Utah • Institute of Theoretical and Experimental Biophysics, Pushchino, Russia • the Nonlinear Research Center, University of Nice • University of Maryland • Ain Shams University, Cairo • Washington University in St. Louis • and last, but back to the beginning, Rainer Hochkoeppler in Basel.

Their work is not unrelated to our subject. With Frank and his distributed lab, we share the belief that the network is a powerful model for understanding natural complexity.

"The brain is basically a large network of interconnected, excitable cells," Frank explained in a message written on his 30th wedding anniversary.[9] "Our interest in excitable cells stems from this observation: within the nervous system, propagation velocity of nerve impulses is rather slow (approx 10 M/sec) or .5 M/sec in cardiac cells. The unit noise is rather high, and the reliability is not really great.

"Compare this with today's computer chips, where propagation velocity is the speed of light, unit noise is almost nonexistent, and reliability is unbelievable.

"Yet the nervous system can perform pattern recognition and computations in many areas much faster than done with the best vector or parallel machines. For me and many others, it's interesting to understand the underlying nature of biological 'networks'—sort of a biological Internet."

While functioning at a high level of performance at low cost, this small group works together around the world yet rarely sees one another. Over time and in its precious face-to-face meetings, the group has developed deep trust.

"Trust is really essential. It's rather easy to do 'ordinary' science or 'ordinary' any job. But to do really creative stuff, it's essential to be absolutely comfortable. Then the creative juices can flow. There are no distractions."

Frank personifies a number of key aspects of *links*.

- The Internet itself represents an astonishing explosion of physical, global communication links and personal access unlike anything available to ordinary human beings before.
- Yet Frank's story is one of relationships grown in the ether of cyberspace, a small group with a global scope and membership. Relationships make the network, but physical links make relationships possible.

- Frank is "networking smart,"[10] deliberately developing fruit-
  ful relationships. Overpublicized as the way to get ahead and
  underappreciated as a skill, networking as an activity is exploding.
- Frank also portrays a new network leadership role—the
  coordinator—whose job is to tend to the network as a whole,
  both online and off.[11]

NETWORKING FALLS TO THE BOTTOM LINE

Underneath all is trust, the soil in which networks grow connections
and relationships.

Trust is the basis of a new source of wealth in the Information Age,
one based on connections. As trust accumulates, people build up
"social capital," which can be turned into economic prosperity just
like land, human, and technology capital.

How does this alchemy come about, this transformation of social
capital into wealth? The answer lies buried nearly a millennium deep,
where odd precursors of the Age of the Network cropped up in the
most unlikely places and times. Not all developments in life are serial;
civilization doesn't evolve in orderly, neat steps. It springs ahead, falls
behind, lurches off strangely, and churns into chaos.

Even though the Middle Ages usually is regarded as an ignorant
time before the great enlightenment, 800 years ago a richly networked
society flourished in northern Italy. Earlier, bands of marauders had
roamed the countryside, terrifying everyone. Feudal lords could not
protect them, so the fledgling middle class came together "to help each
other without fraud and in good faith."[12] The remarkable communal
republics were born, the city-states of Venice, Genoa, Bologna, Milan,
and others, where equality worked and provoked a cultural and
intellectual renaissance.

It's not so much that people banded together in the face of a
common enemy that's amazing. It's what came out of it: economic
prosperity. From trust and abundant social relationships came the

invention of credit, institutions of depository banks, and lending—in short, the ability to use wealth to generate more wealth, the engine of commerce as we know it today.

Because people connected in many ways and trusted one another, their relationships turned into a medieval source of wealth. Eight centuries later, Emilia-Romagna and other northern Italian regions again turned intense relationships into collective wealth and launched the global flexible business network movement.[13]

If it's hard to imagine how trust creates wealth, imagine how its opposite chews up money. Although conventional accounting systems make it hard to calculate the cost of mistrust, the cost is real.[14]

- How much does rework cost when advertising doesn't talk to project managers and engineering doesn't talk to manufacturing?
- What's the price tag on unused inventory sitting in a warehouse because manufacturing, marketing, and sales are engaged in such a fierce war that no one believes anything anyone else says?
- Whose budget is paying for the endless meetings that go nowhere because everyone is afraid to show their cards?
- How much overhead is absorbed in employing people whose only function is to watch over others instead of "doing real work"— the supervisors, inspectors, and enforcers?[15]
- How costly is the miscalculation on receivables that disrupts cash flow and leads to drawing down a line of credit, the interest on which exceeds the time value of lost current dollars?

The solution to all these problems is to build trust, expand communication, and increase links among people, the core capabilities of networks.

FASTEN YOUR SEAT BELT FOR TAKEOFF

The Age of the Network organization needs to be smarter than its predecessors because the ride into the 21st century is going to be very fast indeed. Bureaucracy creates cadres of specialists who know only their particular little bailiwicks. Hierarchy limits access to information with its one-way, top-down stream of command and control. Networks increase communication, multiply information, and bring people into the loop.

Most people want their lives to matter. They want to be part of organizations that engage and learn, where they can see the effect of their achievements, where they have a sense of belonging. It is possible to make a difference in networks, to bring your whole self to work, and to narrow the schism between your "life" and your "work."

Still, networks are hardly without problems. "You asked me about my 'most difficult networking problem,' " wrote (in an e-mail message, of course) Günther Singer, an Austrian automotive consultant who spent the previous five years flattening a multinational company by launching 60 self-managing groups.[16] "It's the power field where two different systems, ideas, or even paradigms meet. It is the tension between the teamnet/virtual project versus the built-for-eternity hierarchy."

There is no organizational nirvana where everyone persists sublimely in eternal harmony. If there were, it would be boring and ineffective. "Networks don't just tolerate conflict," anthropologist Virginia Hine wrote in the 1970s. "They depend on it."[17] Conflict stems from differences of opinion, which are healthy and cause growth.

A story of collaboration and conflict, internal warfare, and kindred communities within high-tech industries gave birth to thousands of companies in the 1980s. People with a new idea that their own company wouldn't fund started another one, from which still another group eventually split, forming its own company, and so on.

Networks allow you to build on what you have. They enhance your relationships with suppliers, anticipate customers' needs, and allow entry to new markets with the competition. *Don't throw out your hierarchy and bureaucracy.* You need them. By clearly defining their places in the organizational universe, you help them to do better what they do best.

TRENDS ON THE HORIZON

The Age of the Network is a harbinger of a pervasive, global organizational shift, a metatrend that points toward other signs close at hand. Keep your eyes on these indicators of the future to help you navigate your journey into the 21st century.

Purpose as a Natural Resource

As radical change prevails for the foreseeable future, organizations will either create their own futures or find themselves reacting to the change driving them. After the wave of interest in reengineering passes, organizations will shift from managing costs to focusing on real business growth. However, it will be tougher than ever to create breakthrough products, enter new markets, and achieve high-performance operations. Facing limits to growth, organizations will reach optimal size, then seek qualitative development rather than quantitative growth. Eventually, people will come to realize that their core business purpose is a natural resource that gives them power in the marketplace.

Focus on People

Team implementations will continue to fail at alarming rates, despite good intentions, unless organizations remove the existing impediments to corporate trust—outmoded reward systems, obsolete status symbols that split people into "haves" and "have-nots," and outdated management practices. Companies will need to reinstill loyalty and motivate their people anew to do incredibly innovative work after downsizing. But eventually, people will rebel against the unending, ever-increasing demand for higher levels of performance.

The Technology of Social Capital

Physical links will continue to explode—from one-to-one to many-to-many—into "digital convergence" at or about the year 2001. Companies will have to learn how to share important information with all employees and some key information with customers and suppliers to be smarter. Just catching up to the learning organization? Rev it up; we'll be moving on to the "fast learning" organization. Before long, people will actively create social capital as a new source of wealth. This dynamic new approach to economic development will begin slowly, then suddenly catch on as success stories accumulate, reaching critical mass at the century's turn.

Everyone a Leader

A new style of leadership is emerging as the old-fashioned, just-do-as-I-say hierarchy fails to perform across company lines. Meanwhile, those to be led are of a different ilk. A new generation of leaders is being groomed that comes from a much more diverse pool, bringing vast cultural differences with them. New jobs and coordinating leadership roles are being invented to manage the burgeoning, bewildering webs of connections and relationships. Not surprisingly, the top will be the last to truly team, and some executives will continue to be embarrassments to their corporate change efforts.

The Strange Benefit of Hierarchy

Layer cutting just for the sake of reducing costs will destroy organizations; a completely flat organization will be equally ineffective. Networks of teams work best across multiple levels. Together, they generate more holistic, integrated views than the single-solution approaches to management, which are on their way out.

The Age of the Network includes all that has gone before, reshapes it, and brings a new spirit and set of capabilities to organizations of every kind and size.

SECTION II

THE BIG IDEA

The next two chapters give the Big Picture: the Age of the Network as the fourth era in the evolution of organization.

By understanding the features of each age, you can understand and benefit from the interplay among small groups, hierarchies, bureaucracies, and networks. It's important because you have to live and work in all these forms simultaneously.

First, in chapter 2, "From Nomads to Networks," you learn about the interplay through a familiar example that contains all forms of organization—the local fire department. Then, in chapter 3, "Turning Hierarchy on its Side," you discover how an exceptional corporation blends the old and new, illustrating the key ideas of each age.

CHAPTER 2

FROM NOMADS TO NETWORKS: THE FOUR AGES OF ORGANIZATION

THE 21ST CENTURY BUCKET BRIGADE

In the past 10 years, the city of Boston has halved its serious fire rate. Likewise, the U.S. rate has dropped by a third. While this is welcome, unexpected public safety news, it carries some surprising pointers for all kinds of organizations.

As government, business, education, nonprofits, and even religions struggle to reinvent themselves, all are reaching for the perfect way to organize. Unknown to the city's 1,570-member fire department, Boston's plummeting rate of multiple-alarm fires holds certain keys to that struggle.

In 1975, the United States had the highest fire rate in the world. Even though it was the world's richest country, with the most sophisticated fire-fighting apparatus, its fire rate was twice that of neighboring Canada. Ironically, countries with the most flammable housing materials, principally in Asia, had some of the lowest fire rates in the world.

There had never been a serious national effort to prevent fires until the mid-1970s. "Only you can prevent forest fires," Smokey the Bear warned, but since most of us didn't live in the forest, this hardly addressed the problems of the South Bronx and South Boston, which were then burning. American children learned the fundamentals of traffic safety but not the basics of fire prevention. Every school child learned to "Look both ways before crossing" but not that "Matches are not for children."

About 20 years ago, Congress passed legislation to create the National Fire Prevention and Control Administration (NFPCA), housed in the Department of Commerce. In 1975, NFPCA inaugurated four major initiatives: improved data collection, arson investigation, training, and fire prevention.

Quite by accident, the Boston area became a hotbed, so to speak, of fire prevention activity. Working with The Children's Museum and our consulting company colleagues, we spent the next three years on national fire prevention education.

In parallel, Boston's Shriners' Burns Institute, Newton's Education Development Center, and the National Fire Protection Association, the trade group also headquartered in Boston that released the 1993 statistics, developed burn prevention programs, the most famous of which were Dick Van Dyke's popular "Stop, Drop, and Roll" TV commercials. They originated in the Boston trade group, funded by the Consumer Product Safety Commission.

Two realizations quickly surfaced when the work began. First, while the fire engine can wail its siren and push traffic aside, fire fighters cannot force people to be fire safe. Fire prevention requires education, not enforcement.

Thus it made no sense to follow the usual federal model: design a program in Washington and ship it out to the field. Instead, we connected the already successful local fire prevention officers across the country. Together we extracted the basic principles of fire prevention education, which we packaged in a variety of print media—from wall charts and comic books to bibliographies and directories. From these materials, local fire fighters were able to adapt their own programs.

The second realization: there was no such thing as a national fire problem. Instead, there were myriad local problems. In Southern

California, as we painfully witness every year, there were brush fires. Chicago—and most other large cities—suffered from a rash of "youthful fire setters." Elderly people in Dade County, Florida, put locks on their doors while placing themselves at risk for quick escape from fire.

In each locale, we found experts—usually fire fighters—who had invented unique, effective, creative programs for their communities.

The startling decline in Boston's fire rate, as well as the nation's, indicates that the 1970s fire prevention effort proved successful over a long time.

"We set a goal to reduce fires in the United States," says Gary Briese, director of the International Association of Fire Chiefs. "We have been more successful than we ever imagined we would be."[1] By "we," Briese, of course, didn't mean his organization alone, but rather implied a massive, largely unrecognized, network of people and groups involved in the overall fire reduction effort.

Surprisingly, fire departments, typically regarded as among the least innovative organizations, turn out to be among the most adaptive for the 21st century.

PUTTING IT ALL TOGETHER

American fire departments incorporate all forms of organization—small groups, hierarchies, bureaucracies, and networks of all sizes.

Fire fighting captures the headlines. The department springs into action as a hierarchy when battling blazes. It prepares for the crisis with command and control and practice and training. If your home erupts in flames, you don't want a group standing around trying to reach a consensus on how to approach the problem. You want someone calling the shots for a highly skilled group of professionals who understand how to deal with heat, chemicals, and combustion out of control.

While fire fighting gets public attention, departments spend only a small part of their time putting out fires (in Boston, only 5 percent). The department acts as a bureaucracy that enforces codes for much of the day and makes certain that pressure is sustained in water lines, that training is updated, and that apparatus is maintained. A chief shouting orders is of very little use if the hydrant isn't pumping. Here you need experts who understand pumps, pressure, and the mechanics of the city water system. Uniform codes fight fires, too.

Fire fighters often use person-to-person networking for fire prevention, which requires education, persuasion, and role models, by working directly with people in the community. School children have no patience for—or need to know about—sprinkler requirements. Their parents need to get the message about the importance of smoke detectors, fire extinguishers, and a second exit from bedrooms. The glamor of a visit to the local fire house and a ride on an engine leave indelible memories in children's minds, but they don't make children fire safe. Commitment to ongoing education does, a distinct and suitable role for networks together with small groups.

Fire departments forge large, interorganizational networks for mutual aid. A group of communities agrees to act as a virtual fire department and back one another up during a particularly bad fire in one locale. Each community gains protection and reduces costs. Here local hierarchies use interlocal networks to achieve something together that they cannot achieve alone. In this field, as in many others, people also use organizational networks to pass legislation, share information, take on large-scale education efforts, and promote professionalism.

All kinds of organizations can learn from the local fire department. In emergencies, command and control prevail. For routine situations and environments, rules and regulations provide standards. Networks educate, innovate, motivate, and provide backup when a hierarchy reaches its limits.

Fire departments—among the oldest of America's institutions and found throughout the world—may be role models for the 21st-century organization.

A SLICE OF TIME

A fire department provides a cumulative "geologic slice" of the evolution of organizations.

Small groups make up the deepest layers. Hierarchy, with its chiefs and sergeants, is the next layer, imposing vertical control. Bureaucracy appears in more recent layers, bringing horizontal specialties. Finally at the top, in the verdant living topsoil, we see intensely linked networks.

Most organizations have mixed forms.

- Ninamary Langsdale's marketing and communications group in the Pittsburgh office of KPMG Peat Marwick works side by side within a few feet of one another and as part of a virtual team scattered from New York to Kentucky to serve an account. Meanwhile, corporate headquarters, home of the hierarchy, is alive and well in New York.

FIRE FIGHTING'S ORGANIZATIONAL SEDIMENTS

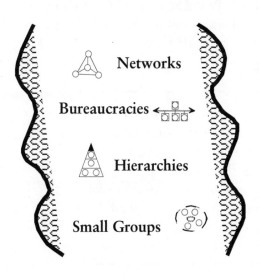

Networks — Mutual aid, professional associations, alliances, distributed sites

Bureaucracies — Codes, inspection, accounting, payroll, maintenance

Hierarchies — Fire fighting, owner-executive decisions, vision, goals, strategy

Small Groups — Education, cross-functional teams, special projects, work groups

Traditional face-to-face small groups continue to be the basic working unit today. At the same time, information-enabled virtual teams cross functions, deliver results to customers, and undertake special projects, while the 100-year-old hierarchy continues to set strategy.

• Chicago's Pritzker family, which owns Hyatt Hotels Corporation, sets the company's long-term goals. The corporation's executives, also concerned with goals, operate the business.

Legitimized by owners, hierarchies provide executive functions. They set goals, maintain authority, and cope with crises, while the senior employees maintain the bureaucracy.

• When an executive at the U.S. Postal Service wanted to bring in experts, a process that could take months, she was able to turn around a purchase order in less than a week.

Although most people complain bitterly about them, bureaucracies, when appropriate and enabling, can be elegantly functional, high-performance entities. They standardize contractual agreements and develop common methods by which work gets done and paid for. This woman knew how to network within the system.

- AT&T Universal Card Services redesigned its core business process in three months by involving people from all levels in the company.

> *In networks, people link as they cross internal functions, geographic boundaries, and even corporate lines with remarkable speed. The people in the network come from the bureaucracy and the hierarchy. Their new relationships to one another create the networks.*

WHAT'S OLD, WHAT'S NEW

All business, indeed, all humanity, is in transition from the Industrial to the Information Age. Alvin Toffler's 1980 book, *The Third Wave*, caught the crest of an idea almost four decades in the making. Now it is conventional wisdom. Three waves divide human history into four great ages characterized by the nomad, agriculture, industry, and information.

FOUR AGES OF ORGANIZATION

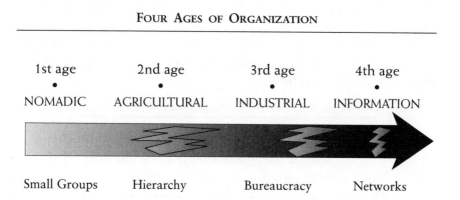

1st age	2nd age	3rd age	4th age
NOMADIC	AGRICULTURAL	INDUSTRIAL	INFORMATION
Small Groups	Hierarchy	Bureaucracy	Networks

> *Each new age of civilization has its signature*
> *form of organization.*

- People first honed their *small group* skills as nomadic hunter-gatherers.
- *Hierarchy* grew up with agriculture.
- The Industrial Age gave birth to *bureaucracy*.
- The Information Age brings *networks*.

A network is a form of organization, like hierarchy and bureaucracy, one of the basic designs we use to construct our social world.

Teamnets of the 21st century span the life of organizational development. Teamnets are at once very old and very new. The team is the small group, rooted in the very old and drawing on skills accumulated over millennia. Networks are the very new, meeting the need for greater scope, speed, and flexibility. They grow at the creative leading edge of change.

WHAT IS YOUR SMALL GROUP?

Thirteen people run IBM's major business units. Five people are on the Executive Committee of the Unitarian Universalist Ministers' Association. Four vice presidents at Qantas Airways ran its reengineering project. Two people own and manage Cafe Appassionato, our local coffee shop.

We have always—and will always—live and work in small groups. Small groups permeate business: microcompanies, small teams in big firms, executive committees.

> *The high-performance, information-enabled,*
> *virtual team is the Age of the Network edition*
> *of the small group.*

Each age adds its special characteristics to the previous one. Small groups are basic social cells that have personalities and identities. People even name them. Small groups carry the seeds of later organizations. As people gain status in new roles and perform tasks, they expand the vertical and horizontal dimensions of organization over the ages.

FROM STATUS TO HIERARCHY

Bill is in Ellen's group. Ellen is on the general manager's staff, which reports to a vice president close to the CEO, who is accountable to the board. In hierarchy, there are many status bands of low, middle, and high ranks with even more grades within them.

Hierarchy dramatically steepens the who's-on-top status dimension in small groups.

As the source of legitimacy in business, owners, who have capital, also bring hierarchy. They officially crown an authority structure of executives and workers.

Hierarchy has helped people build societies among strangers throughout history. As businesses grow beyond the point where everyone knows one another, hierarchies become inevitable.

"Three years ago, all my employees, customers, and suppliers would have fit in this room," said US TeleCenters' CEO, Frank Reece, addressing a few dozen people in one of our workshops. "Now I have 350 employees, thousands of customers, and dozens of suppliers. I can see the bureaucracy growing, and I'm afraid I'm going to create a company I hate."

Every successful entrepreneur bemoans the loss of the "family feeling" as greater size demands structure and formality.

The Egyptian pyramids are the great organizational achievement of the Agricultural Age, the literal eternal symbol for successive ranks culminating in a pinnacle of power. Every time we see a traditional organization chart, the pyramid comes to mind.

Hierarchies alone are not enough. Success brings change, and simple hierarchies are notoriously unstable in the face of the unexpected. Ancient empires rose and fell as populations expanded and capacity became overextended. Boom-bust and on to bureaucracies.

BRING ON THE BOXES: THE BUREAUCRATIC SPECIALTIES

Science ushered in the Industrial Age. Behind logic and the laws of motion chugged the steam engine. Its cargo? Another organizational revolution: rational bureaucracy.

Bureaucracy bulged out sideways with specialized functions, tasks, and roles.

For 300 years, corporations, nations, and organizations of all kinds became more efficient with the organizing prowess of bureaucracy. Bureaucracy, while specializing horizontally, embraced hierarchy, which controlled vertically. Together they managed much greater complexity than either could do alone. The Industrial Age became much more complicated than the Agricultural one.

And the beat continued, faster still. Unfortunately, when faced with continuous uncertainty and change, bureaucracy is like kudzu, the vinelike weed that spreads until it overruns everything and chokes other forms of life. It often creates a new unit to solve a problem, instead of simply connecting people in existing organizations who probably have the answer. Then the "problem" turns into a department.

So a bureaucracy grows, ever bigger, ever slower, until it just sits there, failing to innovate or change, placing drag on everything else. Today's complexity outruns bureaucracy's ability to organize it.

"Only Connect": Linking in Networks

In 1993, worldwide Internet (the global system linking tens of thousands of computer networks) traffic grew at an incredible annual rate of 341,634 percent.[2] A new Internet node—home base for another network of people—joined every 10 minutes; a new person signed on every 30 seconds.

A parallel growth in connections is happening in organizations: alliances are forming at an accelerating rate among firms of all sizes. Services are the economy's growth sector, emphasizing people and process, while manufacturing is shrinking, as agriculture did in the Industrial Age.

Building Capabilities

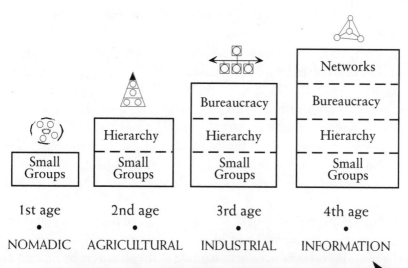

*Connect! It's the organizing imperative of the
Age of the Network.*

Relationships are the dominant reality in the Information Age. They are displacing the focus on matter, which sits at the center of the Industrial Age world view.

Today we are challenged to cope with continuous global change, which constantly presents us with more opportunities. Links—technological and human—drive the reorganization of work. Bureaucracy began horizontal expansion; the Information Age takes it to mach speed.

NETWORK THE ORGANIZATIONAL AGES

What to save? What to change? Where to continue? When to leap ahead?

The complexity that faces 21st-century business outstrips the capacity of the accumulated wisdom of earlier ages. So we invent something new: networks. In the Big Picture, the overall pace of change drives the next form of organization. With new technology eventually comes the ability to manage in an increasingly larger context.

Each age of organization builds upon and includes the past. Networks in particular are inclusive by nature. Breadth gives them resilience; diversity gives them insight; independent members keep them honest.

In the Age of the Network, we still will have hierarchies and bureaucracies, just as we will continue to have farms and factories.

The most literal way networks include earlier forms is by linking all types of organizations.

Members of a network do not themselves have to be networks.

Somerset was the code name for the network that linked Apple, IBM, and Motorola as the three corporate behemoths shared knowledge, talent, and dollars to produce the PowerPC chip. The Strategic Avionics Technology Working Group is the network that links the National Aeronautics and Space Agency (NASA) with its colleagues in industry and the public, as well as with space organizations in other countries, to forge a new vision and working plan for space exploration in the 21st century. Meanwhile, space agencies in the United States, Russia, Japan, and Europe have joined forces in the International Mars Exploration Working Group to "coordinate and work together on future missions to explore the planet Mars."[3]

France, Germany, Spain, and the United Kingdom are bureaucratic partners in Airbus Industrie (whose slogan is "Taking the World

NETWORKS INCLUDE ALL TYPES OF ORGANIZATIONS

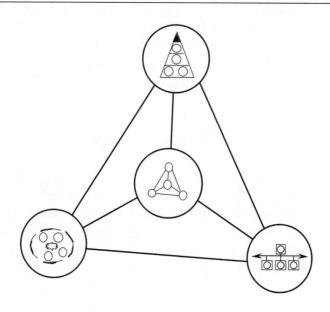

View"), the upstart commercial aircraft manufacturer now controlling 30 percent of the global market.[4] When they work together, hierarchies and bureaucracies naturally form networks yet remain independent.

Different departments in a company often use different organizational forms—quite effectively if they are appropriately tuned to the environment and technology. For example, Nike's fast-moving R&D department is caught up in the latest technologies and networks of professional contacts, and its fleet-footed marketing department interacts intensively with outside agencies, the media, and customers. Finance, however, moves more slowly, calculating along with its bureaucratic, number-processing function. A need for reliable, predictable production capacity leads Nike and its competitors to outsource manufacturing to a network of suppliers, many in Southeast Asia, that may use more rigid, mechanistic structures.

At British Petroleum Exploration (BPX), the procurement department performs a much slower bureaucratic function than the fast-moving, networked world of "frontier exploration" in the Far East. So the entire company lives in a familiar paradox. "It was designed and developed in a world where geography mattered, not where process matters," says Dr. Lilly Evans, a computer scientist and former head of Organizational Engineering for BPX.

To repeat: *all the parts of the network do not have to be the same.* The 21st-century organization comprises all types: small groups, hierarchies, bureaucracies, and networks.

NEW WAYS TO MANAGE

Today, regardless of size, most businesses exist in a global context. Asea Brown Boveri, the Swiss-based $30 billion "multidomestic," operates across more than 100 national borders. Unchanged for 100 years, Halewood Pharmacy, once our neighborhood drug store, suddenly found itself competing with CVS, which suppliers feed from all over the world. Big companies and small cope with global markets and change.

The wave of revolutionary changes catches every business scrambling to survive and position itself to prosper as the fundamental rules of the game change—from our small consulting company to a behemoth the size of General Motors to your company (or nonprofit, government agency, school, denomination, or political party). We all are unavoidably in the storm-wracked passage to a new, expansive, information-based economy.

All around us we see glimpses of the future as we explore the frontiers of markets, technologies, and human performance. Trial and error underlie the slowly accumulating knowledge of what works. You can improve your ability to develop more flexible, faster, and smarter responses by tapping into the expanding pool of experience in teamnets.

THE NEW IN THE NOT SO NEW

Fortunately, the old forms of organization as they currently exist will not mire us forever. We do not have to take all that is oppressive about hierarchy and bureaucracy with us as we speed into the Age of the Network. The Information Age reshapes old forms.

We believe that some hierarchical structure is necessary for any complex, multilevel organization. Hierarchies represent ultimate ownership control and decision making and will continue to do so. However, in the Information Age, networked forms of hierarchies also emerge to fulfill these needs.

Two men sit atop KPMG Peat Marwick, the international accounting firm. A triad including Andy Grove ran Intel for many years. A team of six manages Corning, Inc. A five-person "presidency known as the Operations Committee," whose chair rotates annually, runs AT&T.[5] Conrail's Strategic Manager's Group of 25 runs daily operations. Eastman Chemical Company's plant managers share the manufacturing executive function.

Hierarchy itself is becoming more participatory and diverse in the Information Age. More decisions are being pushed down or out, closer to the work and the customer. We must leave behind something to make this possible—in this case, the narrow, one-way channels of communication and hoarding of information. The nature of control changes with widespread communication and knowledge. Local decision making combines with centralized information sharing in the "network-enabled" hierarchy.

Bureaucracies continue to serve as our legal guardians as specialization remains essential to cope with complexity in the Information Age. Micromanagement, fortunately, will go the way of the dinosaur.

"If the Industrial Revolution gave rise to the gigantic corporate monolith, the Information Revolution will create the 'thousand points of light' of an entrepreneurial culture, where power and creativity are dispersed, decentralized, and democratized," says Bell Atlantic's chairman and CEO, Raymond W. Smith.[6]

Federal Express says that its information system is more valuable than its transportation system. Employees have the power to act at every point of customer contact, supported by a tracking system that is accessible to all. Customers can even get free software from Federal Express to track their own parcels.

At FedEx, bureaucracy becomes an enabling infrastructure rather than a nightmare of bottlenecks.

Some bureaucracies are being transformed rather than replaced. New relationships erupt spontaneously among the departmental boxes as connections multiply. One spectacular example is NetResults, the collection of people-to-people networks that sprang up among federal agencies working on reinventing government (see chapter 6).

OUT OF SIGHT, OUT OF MIND

For most of human history, people were born, lived, and died within walking distance. By definition, a small working group naturally implied that people were physically together—in the popular jargon, collocated. Relationships depended on personal contact in the flesh. Small groups meant face-to-face interactions.

Suddenly, this is no longer true. Just as relationships and the need for coordination explode, so does the geographic distribution of our coworkers. The people we work with are not necessarily in our building, probably not within walking distance, at least not very often.

Proximity breeds coordination and cooperation. People solve problems, the common wisdom goes, by being together physically. If you need a group of people to do something that demands speed and coordination, you have to bring them together.

Now look at the data. Just how close do you have to be to get the advantages of physical proximity? Pretty close.

According to research begun at MIT in the late 1970s,[7] communication rapidly declines as distance increases. MIT Professor Tom Allen studied engineers with offices next door to one another and found that they had a 25 percent probability of communicating at least once a week. Fewer than 10 percent were likely to communicate each week when 30 feet apart. After about 90 feet apart, they were no more likely to communicate than people who were several miles apart.

Another study in the late 1980s[8] focused on how physical proximity affects collaboration. It found that people on the same corridor collaborate five times as often (10.3 percent) as people simply situated on the same floor (1.9 percent). Collaboration drops off sharply again when people occupy different floors (0.3 percent). Ironically, the study found that people in different buildings collaborate slightly more often (0.4 percent) than people on different floors in the same building. You don't think another floor requires a special trip, yet it has the same "out of sight, out of mind" effect.

Steelcase, Inc., the office furniture company, uses this research as a design principle. The "50-foot rule" is the natural size within which collocation leads to collaboration. Unless all the people you work with regularly are near one another, you are part of a distributed virtual group. This makes yours a "special needs organization" when it comes to being explicit about communication and collaboration.

Welcome to the world of networked work.

The Information Age dramatically alters space and time. We no longer need to be in the same place to connect. Communications channels and up-to-date information are no longer scarce resources.

Connectivity is exploding, yet face-to-face encounters account for most of our small-group knowledge. Historically, hierarchical authority, in particular, has depended on the power of personal characteristics, the power of the person, the body—the Big Guy with the booming voice and displays of power, as well as power settings, to maintain control.

It's hard to bring physical bearing to bear when you're communicating by e-mail. All the CAPITAL LETTERS and !@#$* characters (denoting indignation and the like) on the computer screen can't compare with someone on a power trip staring you down. Physical qualities and locations are less important in the ephemeral age now unfolding. We are learning new, more horizontally connected, participatory ways of achieving higher levels of small-group performance.

So, alongside the old, the new. Thanks to the field of organization development, we are rediscovering ancient small-group, face-to-face knowledge. At the same time, we're inventing some brand new skills for the geographically spread groups of the 21st century.

ON A PERSONAL LEVEL

We all belong to many different groups simultaneously. Moving from group to group, we can travel through the ages.

A fire fighter can stride through all four ages in a single work day.

Upstairs over the station house is a small world with a kitchen, rec room, and bunks where the informal small group sleeps, a very placid environment—until the alarm goes off. Then the informal group dons its firefighting gear, snaps into a military unit, and heads for the crisis. After the fire, the fighter puts on a bureaucratic uniform and becomes an inspector to assess the damage and investigate the cause. That night, the uniform comes off and a person with a mission to save lives joins with a network of teachers and other leaders working to prevent fires in the community.

Useful, timeless basic human capabilities recur in each new age. Our life is a mosaic of past and future. Each of us, like the fire fighter, exists simultaneously in all four ages.

The new postindustrial model is *inclusive* of old models, not *replacements* for them. The laws of motion in everyday life did not grind to a halt when quantum physics overwhelmed Newtonian absolutes at the dawn of the 20th century; the experience of gravity did not change when Einstein discovered relativity.

Each age makes a contribution to the repertoire of human organizations, with older forms gaining new features in later ages. Yet core patterns remain, and our challenge is to know which pattern to apply where.

CHAPTER 3

TURNING HIERARCHY ON ITS SIDE: HOW SMART ORGANIZATIONS KEEP THE BABY AND THROW OUT THE BATH WATER

EASTMAN: A TEAMNET COMPANY

Once, when "going West" meant trekking across the Appalachian and Allegheny mountains, Kingsport in eastern Tennessee was a doorway to the colonial frontier. Today, home to Eastman Chemical Company, it is the new outpost of the 21st-century Information Age organization.

Eastman, as it is known, is big and old, and in a dirty industry. If you think in stereotypes, you'd be hard pressed to consider it an ideal teamnet enterprise. Put your stereotypes aside. Eastman is a premier example of what can happen when a company networks itself from top to bottom. In 1993, it received the U.S. "Nobel" for quality, the Malcolm Baldrige National Quality Award.

Eastman offers lessons for networked organizations everywhere. It especially answers questions asked by many old-line organizations in traditional industries: Can we change? Can we transform ourselves from old to new without ripping everything out and starting over? Will it be worth it?

This story offers hope and inspiration. But remember this: it is no quick fix.

EASTMAN'S STORY

George Eastman founded his chemical company in 1920 to provide an independent supply of chemicals for his photography business. Although big by other standards, Eastman Chemical Company remained a medium-sized player in an industry of giants. When the company loaded 80 of its employees, some of whom had never flown before, onto a plane to go to Washington, D.C., to accept the Baldrige Award, it was the 10th largest chemical company in the United States and 34th in the world, with 17,750 employees and $4 billion in sales.

Times were not always so good. In the late 1970s, the company was in crisis: a major product line was losing market share. The reason? Poor quality.

To solve the problem, they initiated a focused quality improvement effort. Results were dramatic: customer complaints plummeted to less than one-tenth their previous level as manufacturing costs dropped; productivity increased and market share expanded.

This is where many quality improvement stories end. Flush with victory, successful executives feel they have a winning formula for handling the next crisis. No need to make big changes.

Not at Eastman. This is where things began. In 1982, they started a companywide Customer Emphasis Program. Within a year, they had crafted their original "Quality Policy," the first of four "foundation" documents still in use as guiding principles a decade later. Within two years, customers were coming into the plants and joining the improvement efforts, heralding a major reversal of both corporate policy and tradition.

The company formed teams at all levels beginning in the mid-1980s, which ultimately proved to be the critical defining element in Eastman's success.

"We do all our work in teams," Bob Joines, Eastman's vice president of quality, says.

By taking a hard look at their culture, they realized how many of their internal practices were barriers to teamwork (see chapter 8). So, they removed them, paving the way to write "The Eastman Way," their second foundation document, which serves as the "people pillar" of their philosophy.

They took another big leap forward in 1986 when they developed their Quality Management Process (QMP). QMP provided a common language and process for teams at all levels to use, starting with the team at the top. Senior executives had to "walk their team talk." They began to set clear goals, which they call "major improvement opportunities."

They applied for the Baldrige for the first time in 1988. They hoped to win, of course, but they also used the application process to drive their growing efforts to pay more attention to customers, to empower and offer development opportunities for employees, and to spawn new relationships with suppliers. They didn't win on the first round, but by using the Baldrige Award criteria for internal measures, senior management again worked to refine the corporate vision and mission.

In 1991, Eastman published their third foundation document, "Strategic Intent," and, in 1993 it adopted their fourth pillar, "Responsible Care."® An industry alliance developed this set of commitments to health, safety, and the environment,[1] reflecting a codification of Eastman's already exemplary record in these areas.

Results of more than a decade's work are impressive. Seventy percent of their customers around the world rate Eastman as their No. 1 supplier. The company has reduced quality-related claims and returns due by 35 percent and achieved a shipping reliability of nearly 100 percent for four years. As the pace of change quickens, Eastman kept up by reducing its time to market 50 percent from 1990 to 1993 and churning innovation into 22 percent of sales with products five years of age or less.

Eastman is an Information Age company. Management, not product, puts them at the leading edge of the transitional wave. What gives them their organizational advantage? Use the teamnet principles to see.

LOOKING THROUGH THE TEAMNET GLASSES

As a whole, Eastman is a "network of interlocking teams,"[2] says Bob Joines. In our terms, Eastman has developed teamnets, not only in name and theory, but in practice. They exist not only in a department or division, but throughout the entire company.

"How do we get everyone engaged for alignment?" Joines asks. "We start at the top, with CEO Earnie Deavenport and the 11-member Executive Team. Everyone is a member of interlocking teams across the levels. We have 800 or 900 of them. But they're not the only teams we've got. We also have 500 to 600 cross-functional teams. This is where the real work gets done."

These are only the named, official teams. Thousands more exist informally in a culture of high trust and considerable clarity about shared purposes.

Purpose

When Eastman hit its market wall in 1979, it found a clue about where to go to discover the source of its business purposes—its customers. "We started asking and still do ask, 'who are our customers and what do they need?' " Joines says.

Since then, Eastman has maintained a close vigil on its customers. Every team focuses on its customers, both internal and external. Eastman's QMP and its common team methodology add a vital assessment step between customers and the "plan–do–check–act" quality improvement cycle. To assess its customers and its reason for existence, each Eastman team develops its vision and mission, along with specific results and ways to measure them.

This process begins at the top, Joines explains. Complete participation by senior management, along with the interlocking team structure, has enabled the development and deployment of common purposes throughout the company. Operations connects with vision at Eastman. They translate abstract business theories into pragmatic realities.

In "Strategic Intent," its vision statement, Eastman sets out "to be the world's preferred chemical company." The mission is "to create superior value" for five sets of stakeholders: customers, employees, investors, suppliers, and the public.

The strategy focuses on "exceeding customer expectations" while achieving "major improvement opportunities, the annual goals." With goals in hand, organizations throughout Eastman develop "strategic alternatives." Teams develop alternatives as "supporting projects," which they include in the annual plan.

Every project team understands its connection to the strategic intent, where the real legitimacy for its work resides.

Everyone participates in building the plan as a whole, which senior management takes responsibility for guiding.

Members and Levels

Teams within teams within teams. In a large enterprise teamnet like Eastman, people belong to multiple levels of internal teams, as well as a variety of external partnership teams.

At Eastman, each member of the top team represents both an organization and a team made up of members who themselves lead organizations. This is the strategy of "interlocking" teams. Everyone is line. There are no staffs.

"Each team," says Joines, "has its own understanding of the mission and purpose. They know who their customers are and what their key success factors and result areas need to be. Each team creates measures of performance over time."

People make up human organizations the way parts make up machines. Eastman involves everyone. This pragmatic approach to employee empowerment rests on a basic belief in people.

To be successful, people need knowledge, skills, and education, along with authority. They cannot take responsibility and act for the good of the customer and the company without authority. "We need people to feel like owners of our enterprise," Joines says.

The paragraph on teamwork in "The Eastman Way" combines the independence empowerment offers with the compensating focus on unifying purpose:

> *"We are empowered to manage our areas of responsibility. We work together to achieve common goals for business success. Full participation, cooperation, and open communication lead to superior results."*

Ideology, or "the way things have always been done," does not prevent Eastman from changing what needs to be changed. "We had to get rid of some structural impediments to teams," Joines says. They pushed considerable decision-making authority down the vertical chain of command. They have pushed down salary decisions, in particular, to the working units (see chapter 8), providing a powerful, practical source of autonomy and responsibility.

Eastman also partners with both customers and suppliers. Some 40 customer–partner teams (representing 80 percent of their business) and 42 supplier teams[3] cap extensive cross-boundary interactions with businesses at both ends of their value-creation system, inputs and outputs.

Leaders and Links

"We rotate leadership at the highest level," Joines responds when asked how Eastman handles leadership.

Rotating leadership is a fact of life at Eastman: the company sets out to empower people, enabling all to lead when desired or necessary. "We set out principles and guidelines rather than prescriptions," Joines says. Leaders on one team are members of another. In this way, leadership multiplies and expands rather than becoming exclusive and hoarded.

Joines estimates that high-performing cross-functional teams have cut the number of traditional first-line supervisors by almost a third. When you focus on the work, unneeded areas of bureaucracy naturally wither away.

Senior management is the citadel of hierarchy and the last bastion of traditional control. Yet here, too, Eastman pushes the frontier with a number of very senior teams. A team of five, comprising the presidents of the manufacturing facilities, manages the manufacturing function. Leadership rotates every quarter. The senior administrative team also self-manages. Leadership in core competencies, such as Polymer Technology, Organic Chemical Synthesis Technology, and Site Management, is even more distributed. The 12 market-focused business organizations, however, look somewhat more traditional: they cluster in two teams led by executive vice presidents, the same design used for the Worldwide Business Support team.

All teams meet regularly, usually every week or two. Extensive communications systems—phone, fax, e-mail (which Joines describes as "pervasive"), telephone conference calls, newsletters, events, and more—support a culture of open information and access.

Physical links offer an opportunity to interact with others, but without relationships among the people, the physical links are meaningless. People at Eastman expect direct, cross-boundary communication; it is the norm.

"Feedback from the Baldrige examiners described us as a 'seamless' organization," comments Joines. "We absolutely promote horizontal communication and expect it to go that way. There is no formal system of hand slapping. We're not doing skunkworks; rather, what we're engaged in is open and supported."

"The Eastman Way" lays out the values that are enunciated and explained in the company: honesty and integrity, fairness, trust, teamwork, diversity, employee well-being, citizenship, and a winning attitude. Trust underlies even the norm of horizontal communication. It is the deeper foundation that Eastman worked on early and comes back to often. Here is the true nutrient soil of beneficial relationships.

TURNING THEORY INTO PRACTICE

"In order to make changes," says Joines at the very start of our first interview, "Theory is key. Unless we understand the applicable theory and are convinced it's right, [it's] no go." He is talking not just about the technology systems, but also, and especially, about the social system. "We are clearly driven by business needs, fundamentally survival. To be successful, we have to come to grips with the social side. We won't make it without every employee's hands on the plow."

Eastman engages in active social science in pursuit of business goals. Theory is the source for innovations—hypotheses—that are tested, revised, and retested until a sufficiently high level of confidence is reached and the change is embraced. Pilots and prototypes provide valuable laboratory results to inform large-scale implementation strategies.

General guidelines develop from theory to replace detailed rules. Many leaders can make localized decisions yet produce overall coherence.

Eastman reflects all the basic teamnet principles, demonstrating how a theory of network organization and an evolutionary model of accumulating capabilities work in the real world.

THE INEVITABLE USE OF HIERARCHY

Now let's see how hierarchy fits into the picture. But this view of hierarchy is different from the usual one. It's about organization instead of power—how the right design gives competitive advantage. To illustrate, we adapt one of the most famous parables of general systems theory, that of the two Swiss watchmakers, first told by the Nobel Prize-winning economist Herbert Simon, who called them Tempus, meaning "smooth time," and Hora, meaning "serial time."[4]

THE INNOVATORS

Two young technologists, feeling the limits of their then crude craft, began to develop breakthrough products for their market. Soon, both developed splendid prototypes of awesome versatility and complexity. Indeed, Sam Serial, the pride and joy of the traditional masters in the field, finished his model noticeably sooner than Laura Levels, the challenger of orthodoxy. Clearly, Sam had the edge in what could be a very big market. The business press eagerly looked forward to the unfolding story.

News of the revolutionary demos spread, and people started to call for information, interrupting the young entrepreneurs with questions. Within a few months, Laura was delivering to delighted customers, while Sam struggled to complete the first production copy as orders piled up. Both decided to hire apprentices and to train new workers in their respective methodologies to meet the demand. Laura was able to train new people quickly and boost production enormously, while Sam sank further into the mud as training crawled and products only occasionally appeared.

After Sam Serial's bankruptcy, the observers began to investigate to learn what they could from this epic story of success and failure. The key difference, they discovered, was in how each designed the work of constructing the product—the organizational advantage.

Sam simply extended the "Old Way" of fitting pieces together into a whole by adding many more pieces. The effect was somewhat like a rich mosaic, a thousand parts put together intricately, just so— a beautiful but fragile assembly.

Laura, however, borrowed a method from nature and constructed a series of subassemblies, 10 pieces to a group, intermediate components of the product. The extra steps spent putting subassemblies together accounted for the initially longer time needed to build the prototype. This integrated approach produced a design both elegant and resilient.

When assembly is interrupted, the partially completed unit is put down and naturally it falls a-*part*. It dis-*assembles*. What works well in isolation does not always work well in the real world that is full of interruptions—otherwise known as change. For each thousand steps of process, Sam risked hundreds of steps at every interruption, while Laura lost only an average of five steps when she resumed the assembly process. Laura had designed "stable clusters" between the elementary pieces and the product as a whole, specific points in the process that held together without the next step.

The power of Laura's method of chunks within chunks became clear as volume increased and markets changed. Laura Levels, with a probability of just one interruption per 100 steps, gained a 4000-to-1 advantage over Sam Serial.

Such is the power of hierarchy of the scientific sort. Simon called this pattern the "architecture of complexity."

PUTTING PIECES OF COMPLEXITY TOGETHER

Systems within systems within systems. Why is this design principle so universal and so powerful?

Simon said that complexity evolves much more rapidly from simplicity if there are "stable intermediate structures," subsystems sturdy enough not to pull apart. Hierarchies predominate in nature, he said, because "hierarchies are the ones that have the time to evolve."

This is a profound, basic, natural design principle: a hierarchy of levels.

Add levels to your understanding of hierarchy; it's more fundamental than the social power structure that you usually mean when you refer to hierarchy.

In the scientific sense of levels, hierarchy is basic to astronomy: planets and satellites in solar systems in galaxies in galaxy clusters that are part of superclusters and even greater amalgamations. Hierarchy brings us molecules, atoms, particles, and quarks in physics. Biology has cells, tissues, organs, organisms, ecologies, and environments. Pennies make up dimes that make up dollars in the U.S. currency system. Time comes in subassemblies of minutes, hours, days, weeks, months, and years. Libraries shelve books according to the Dewey Decimal System version of this theme. We even build our community communications systems this way with trunks, feeders, and drop lines to the house.

Levels within levels—hierarchies—permeate every aspect of the core technology of the Information Age.

Computer hardware is built in levels—from binary switches to chips to logic boards to computers to systems with peripherals. We design software in levels of complexity from machine languages to assemblers to operating systems to applications; structure files hierarchically, whether in DOS directories or Mac folders; and connect PCs in local area networks plugged into wide area networks linked to the global Internet.

We use the hierarchy principle every time we analyze a problem or break something complex into smaller parts. We also use it to put things together, for synthesis, to create new wholes out of parts. When we outline our thinking, we use hierarchy.

It is no surprise, then, that the same level structure permeates organizations. As individuals, we are parts of families who make up communities and neighborhoods, which in turn are included in local, state, and national jurisdictions. All of these are points of natural cleavage—stable intermediate forms, as Simon says—in the hierarchy of society.

> *All networks are hierarchical. Even the simplest ones are made up of interacting parts that are themselves complex—people or companies, for example.*

Interruption is a metaphor for change in the story of the inventors, Laura Levels and Sam Serial. The need to organize in stable clusters, modules, and levels increases as the pace of interruption picks up. Subassemblies—distinct components that can stand on their own— become more necessary, while rigid control structures become liabilities under the unrelenting push of ever-increasing change.

Networks do not throw the baby out with the bath water. They directly incorporate the powerful principle of hierarchy in its timeless sense—*the force behind stable clusters*—into the organizational form of networks, a key legacy of the Agricultural Age of hierarchy.

THINKING THE NETWORK WAY

To cope with more complexity, groups have to be smarter. Each epoch has brought a new level of organizational intelligence required to meet its challenges. Group intelligence lies in a group's actual organization, in how it does its work. Over time, the capacity for group intelligence has increased.

New ages in human civilization bring new configurations, new patterns, to organizations. As the organizational repertoire increases, groups of all sizes have the potential for even greater intelligence. Even a small increase in the average intelligence of our groups has an enormous impact on our collective ability to solve the problems of the world.

TEAMNET PRINCIPLES ACROSS THE AGES

To understand what's going on around us, we use mental models of the world.

Each new era brings a shift from one dominant world view to another. When the industrial view prevailed over the agricultural one, and both over the "precivilized" hunting-gathering world, the new patterns were seen as replacing the old ones, if not destroying them. But:

The Age of the Network includes *rather than replaces its predecessors.*

Quantum physics doesn't regard Newtonian mechanics as absolutely wrong, but rather as relatively limited. In the same way, bureaucracy is not wrong; it's just limited. Indeed, it *should* be limited to those functions for which it is most appropriate.

We use simple social models for simple organizations: informal small groups or simple hierarchies. Few situations are more absurd (or boring) than those in which a very small group of people adheres to Robert's Rules of Order. We've all been to those meetings (and sometimes run out screaming).

More complex situations call for more complex models. Until recently, our only response has been to structure multilevel hierarchies bursting with internal bureaucracies. Their rigidity is as maladaptive in the Age of the Network as Sam Serial's sequential manufacturing process.

> *Today's dramatically increased, complex pace*
> *of change calls forth new designs—teams and*
> *networks together.*

Because it is inclusive, the network is also compatible with earlier forms of organization. Networks can describe all types of organizations, including hierarchies, which are special cases of the more general network form.

Each age has made an essential contribution to the evolving organizational model reflected in the Five Teamnet Principles (see chapters 4 and 5).

- The Nomadic Age provided the basic idea of *members* defining *boundaries.*
- The Agricultural Age contributed the concept of *level* structure.
- The Industrial Age offered up the precision of *specialized purpose.*
- And the Information Age contributes explosive-in-number *links* that cross boundaries, levels, specialties, cultures, places, industries, jurisdictions, politics, religions, and every other difference important to people.

SITTING AROUND THE CAMPFIRE: SMALL-GROUP BOUNDARIES

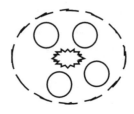

In the Nomadic Age, people formed tribes, multifamily groups of individuals who offered one another a survival advantage over being alone. Nowhere is the systems truism "The whole is greater than the sum of its parts" more evident than when a group emerges from the association of individual people. The principle of "greater than" arises from relationships among the members. At this scale, you can "feel" synergy.

Groups come to life all the time. A group that lasts has "clicked" at some point in its development, a new "whole" born with the first unconscious use of the term "we." People just *know* when a group is a group and when it is not.

The members of a group define its boundary, which means that if membership is not clear, then neither is the boundary. Small groups and networks alike are apt to have fuzzy "dotted-line" boundaries. Their boundaries clarify and then blur, unlike the sharper, exclusionary, in-or-out "solid-line" boundaries of hierarchy and bureaucracy.

The center of a small group is magnetic. As nomads, the group sat and lived around the camp fire, with those closest to the heat forming the inner circle. Then came the outer circle and finally the camp 'perimeter—the boundary.

In the language of the network, individuals are members, rimmed by a boundary, that can be fuzzy or distinct. This fundamental design is basic for teams of all ages at all levels.

PYRAMID POWER: CLIMBING THE HIERARCHICAL LEVELS

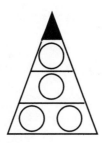

Mention the word "hierarchy" and few people will cheer. But this often dreaded word brings into social use one of nature's basic organizing patterns—levels. Everything complex is part of more complex things that are made up of parts that are themselves even more complex.

Hierarchy, in the scientific use of the term, is a fundamental cross-boundary systems principle.

Nowhere is it more important to be able to separate the conceptual contribution from its historical development. An unfortunate terminological quirk has made it difficult to bring this critical systems idea to the area that needs it most: the complex social world.

"Hier-archy" literally means "priestly rulership." While science easily sheds the theological nuances to reach the universal clarity underneath, this is not so easy in organizations.

The *level* structure of nature is the "baby" in the "bath water" of traditional hierarchy. Inclusive levels do *not* imply one-way information flow and top-down control in nature. There each level has its regularities, its appropriate scales of space and time.

It is critical to separate the powerful principle of levels from the characteristic of vertical control that is part of hierarchy's social meaning. Networks retain the "architecture of complexity" through the principle of integrated levels.

THE SYSTEMS WE LOVE TO HATE: BUREAUCRACIES
WITH A PURPOSE

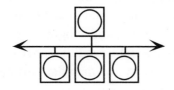

Bureaucracy and hierarchy (in the social sense) have a lot in common. Both laud rank. Bureaucracy, however, draws its legitimacy from a different source. It looks to the law where the top-down, one-way control hierarchy uses coercive force. No matter how much you hate bureaucracy, legality is a vast improvement over the brute force, "might makes right" legitimacy of hierarchy that prevailed in the Agricultural Age.

The Industrial Age's great contribution to organization is specialization. Horizontal bureaucracy offers great strength when combined with vertical hierarchy. It provides a rational process for spreading out work. Thus, bureaucracies are able to achieve much larger and more stable social structures than hierarchy alone.

A sense of purpose is central to people and organizations of all ages. Bureaucracy makes purpose explicit. It is formal, and it serves as the ultimate rationale. Bureaucratic constitutions and charters begin with the organization's purpose.

For example, the first words of the Preamble to the U.S. Constitution establish this country's purpose and set some goals: "We the People of the United States, in Order to form a more perfect Union, establish Justice, insure domestic Tranquility, provide for the common defence, promote the general Welfare, and secure the Blessings of Liberty to ourselves and our Posterity, do ordain and establish this Constitution for the United States of America." Such "in order to" statements are formal and serve as the ultimate authority. Organizations "get a life" for a reason. They divide and manage work in pursuit of a goal.

Specialization allows an organization to define work at all levels. Since there are infinite ways to chop up work, this is where the group's competitive IQ develops. The smarter it is, the better the group is at dividing and integrating the right chunks of work. This is unavoidable creative work for every group, recognized or not.

Time is continuous, smooth, and progressive in the industrial world view; ideally, it is serial. Serial time, like Newtonian physics, provides an excellent model of reality for many situations. We use it spontaneously to plan our everyday activities:

Thinking ahead to a cup of coffee, I start from my office, go through a linear sequence of steps to the kitchen, more steps to make the coffee, and wait for it to go through its steps, one by one, to reach the goal—a cup of coffee.

We often "chunk work" in a literal picture of a serial process. Businesses with a goal of developing and delivering products to customers, for example, create functions that mimic it: marketing and R&D, design and production, and sales and service, corresponding to the beginning, middle, and end of the process.

The merits of analytic specialization are well known, as are its limits. By dividing up work, people achieve more together than each person can alone doing all the steps in sequence. But too much specialization fragments reality and imposes an immense control-coordination burden.

At the bottom of the rational bureaucratic tree, work is "Taylored"[5] into standardized units suitable for the mechanized time of mass production. Specialties and repetitive, sequential steps that may be fine in moderately paced change environments begin to proliferate uncontrollably in turbulent environments requiring rapid adaptation. In this environment, complexity limits purely analytic solutions.

In networks, the principle of unifying purpose plays the same role as goal-oriented specialization does in bureaucracy. The focus on purpose in a network is more intense because it is the primary source of legitimacy, it holds members together voluntarily. Successful networks articulate their purposes explicitly and express them as useful plans and activities.

THE TIES THAT BIND: NETWORK LINKS

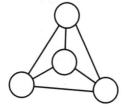

Links stand for all sorts of human connections—similarities, communications, relationships—and have always been with us.

Links are very simple when you consider each link on its own, one by one. But even a few links connected together form distinctive patterns, and complexity expands rapidly as the number of links grows.

Relationships among people and groups develop over time through interaction. Technologies that provide new media for interaction have been leading-edge drivers of change throughout the ages. New technologies provide new opportunities for new interactions that, over time, enable new relationships and organizations.

Spoken communication among people helped inaugurate the first age of civilization, and each age added new capabilities—writing in the Agricultural Age, printing in the Industrial Age, and electronic communication in the Information Age.

For most of history, links among people that reached beyond personal connections have been scarce and costly. Links are formal, tagged with one-way signs, and relatively few in traditional hierarchies and bureaucracies.

Boom! Links explode in number in the Information Age as our personal reach suddenly goes global. We complete the loop by being able to talk to anyone anywhere at any time. The vertical frontier closes as organizations become massively interconnected in all directions, and we catapult into the Age of the Network.

We dramatically increase the need to manage greater complexity in the horizontal dimension as we reach the limits of vertical hierarchy. We do so not by adding more specialities but, instead, by creating more links.

In the Information Age, links are much more numerous and more real than in past ages. Many more people and technologies serve linking roles and functions now than in the past.

Massive linking allows decentralized, individual access to centralized, shared information. This increases decentralized decision making following a centralized strategy. Links give the network its basic benefits, the best of both centralized and decentralized worlds:

- Flexibility,
- Speed, and
- Power.

Networks provide the flexibility of pulling together what's needed when it's needed; the speed of multiple decision makers with authority who operate from common values and plans; and the power that comes from close links among independent members.

Successful networks bring great benefits. But links alone do not a smart network make. A profusion of unrelated links brings only confusion.

The true intelligence of a group lies in how it configures itself. Its configuration comes from the pattern of relationships as a whole, and the smartest organizations constantly reconfigure to fit more complex environments and changing purposes.

Links connect all the teamnet principles: members and leaders within and across boundaries, across levels, and across purposes. All the elements together lead to the network—the Organizing Pattern of the Age of the Network.

WINDS OF CHANGE

How does the idea of a small group expand over time? A simple abstract allegory, almost a cartoon, illustrates how the ideas come together as a group enlarges, accumulates capabilities, and becomes more complex.

In the mostly command-and-control vertical hierarchy (in the social sense), power flows from top to bottom. The organization chart has height, with very narrow breath of expertise. The effect is like a two-dimensional cutout. Hierarchies, while tall, imposing, and quite successful when the pace of change is slow, easily blow over as the winds of change increase. Just look at the "boom-bust" cycles of the ancient agricultural hierarchies from Egyptian to Mesopotamian to Mayan.

Now add bureaucracy. The result is a much more stable arrangement. By metaphorically putting hierarchy and bureaucracy together, we get a "stool." A stool, standing upright, with feet spread apart, is quite useful and sturdy. It provides horizontal support for the up-down dimension.

CHANGE HITS THE TOWERING HIERARCHY

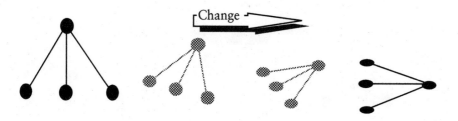

MORE CHANGE TOPPLES HIERARCHY-BUREAUCRACY

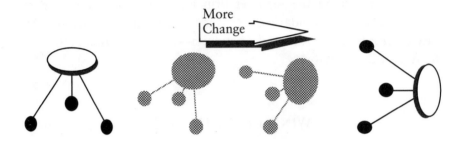

The stool is likely to tip over, however, when big winds of change blow from unexpected directions. If it does not have the right orientation, the hierarchy-bureaucracy stool becomes useless. Since the feet aren't tied together, pressure on the top of the stool can easily cause it to collapse.

Now add links among the groups at the base of the stool's legs. When you connect all the organization's fundamental parts, you create an enormously strong structure, symbolized here by the tetrahedron, which the visionary architect R. Buckminster Fuller called the universe's minimal closed structure.

To convert a hierarchy-bureaucracy to a network, just add links.

FAST CHANGE SPINS THE NETWORK

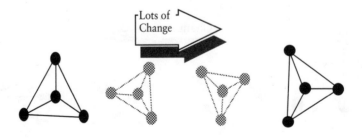

Different orientations in a network may be called top or bottom, periphery or center, or, perhaps most appropriately, foreground and background. Here we symbolize the leadership of networks, foreground representatives of the whole. Different parts of the organization, different leaders, come to the fore as the winds of change whip through the environment.

Tumbling quickly through time, networks seem to take on a spherical shape. They are always right side up.

TURNING TREES INTO WHEELS

There are other ways to show levels besides the familiar top-down tree chart. You also can represent hierarchy horizontally.

Instead of trees, think of wheels. A tree's top and bottom are

HIERARCHICAL LEVELS IN TREES AND WHEELS

Tree   **Wheel**

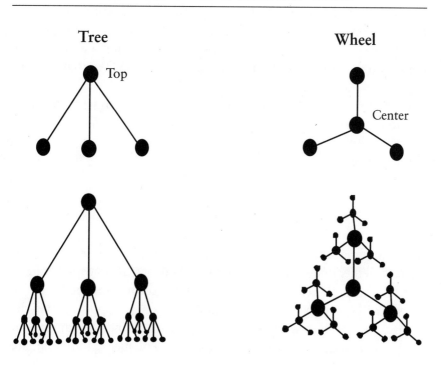

functionally equivalent to a wheel's center and periphery. Superior-subordinate roles in trees have corresponding hub-subhub roles in wheels. Both arrangements reflect the same logic of hierarchical levels.

The difference, of course, comes in the use of links. Vertical, one-way connections constrict information flow, while two-way hub-and-spoke communications provide control and coordination opportunities. To convert a wheel to a network, just add links (as in the previous diagram, above, that shows the network tetrahedron).

THE FOUR-DIMENSIONAL EASTMAN ORGANIZATION

Eastman used a truly cross-sectional approach in showing how its hierarchy, bureaucracy, and network fit together in a 21st-century organization. The central and foreground position of the Chairman and CEO, Earnie Deavenport, symbolizes hierarchy. Structurally, his position anchors the hub-and-spoke locations of the six major corporate components. Bureaucracy is well represented both in the general use of specialization and purpose—every subgroup has a unique name and mission—and in specific components devoted to maintaining traditional bureaucratic functions.

Eastman created "four matrixed dimensions"[6] to accomplish its mission effectively:

- Functions
- Core competencies
- Geographies
- Business organizations

Two components embrace the bulk of Eastman's bureaucracy, collected together under a Functional Management team and an Administration and Staff team. Core Competency Teams comprise a loose network of specialty clusters. Worldwide Business Support serves the various geographies while Eastman's 12 basic business organizations (such as Fibers, Container Plastics, and Polymer Modifiers) are

EASTMAN CHEMICAL COMPANY'S ORGANIZATION CHART

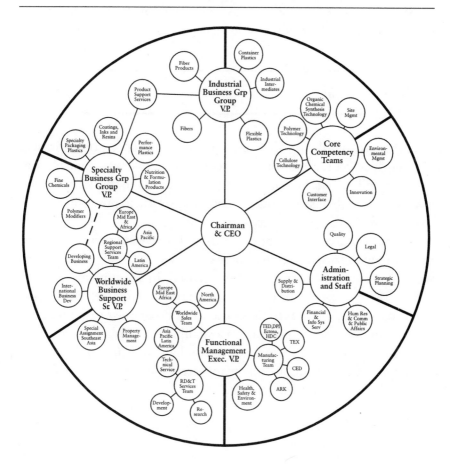

grouped into two components, Specialty Business and Industrial Business.

What makes the Eastman chart so uniquely indicative of an Information Age networked organization is its periphery. This heavy outer circle attaches directly to all the major components and represents the direct connections among the departments. Deavenport talks about the "white space," where, according to Joines, "we don't have writing; that's where collaboration takes place and work gets done." In the circle, he repeats, "no one is on top."

The thicker outer line is intentional. "The circle around the whole is the superhighway that connects us," explains Joines. This circle symbolizes how the whole coheres through links.

Add links.

These two words are the fundamental formula for transforming existing hierarchies and bureaucracies into networks—human connections and physical communication links. Let the specialized organizations sort themselves out by focusing on their purpose and the work needed to achieve global corporate goals.

"Work gets done across and within and between functions. Major processes in the organization have to go horizontal. A lot of important work doesn't get done in the vertical sense," Joines explains.

Still, there's a place for hierarchy, he says. "Sometimes Earnie [the Chairman and CEO] has to make decisions no one else can. You can't stamp out hierarchy and run an organization. You have to have vertical alignment. To be successful, you have to learn to do both of these together. Our interlocking teams are a hierarchy in a sense, and then we *turn hierarchy on its side.*"

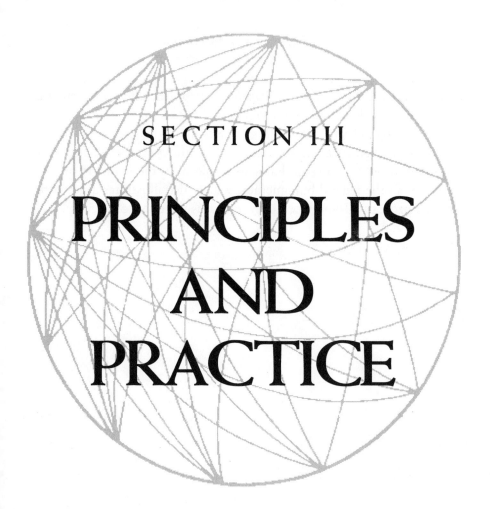

SECTION III

PRINCIPLES AND PRACTICE

In this "how to" section the big ideas are put into practice, using networks as an explicit type of organization that operates according to certain principles.

In chapter 4, "A Pocket Tool for Teamnets," you learn the Five TeamNet Principles, where to apply them, and how to avoid failure along the size scale from small to megagroups. More on the principles appears in *The TeamNet Factor*, especially chapters 2–7, where we also devote two chapters to small business networks, here represented by the story of Harry Brown's EBC Industries.

In chapter 5, "Rx for Monday Morning," you learn to apply the principles at different phases of the network's life to assess and plan small but complex groups—from the executive suite to the shop floor to the neighborhood. More information on process and practice appears in chapters 8–10 of *The TeamNet Factor* (including a systematic work process design methodology with associated planning tools).

Finally, in chapter 6, "The Hinge of History," you shift from operations to strategy, taking assessment and planning up a level. Contrast your situation with a remarkable example from the frontiers of networking in the federal bureaucracy, which also illustrates a network launch process. "To network or not; that is the question."

CHAPTER 4

A POCKET TOOL FOR TEAMNETS: APPLYING THE FIVE PRINCIPLES AT ALL LEVELS

BOLTING INTO THE FUTURE

In 1993, Pennsylvania's Erie County Economic Development Council named Harry Brown "Employer of the Year." Brown is one of the most successful teamnet executives in the United States, though his company may not fit your image of the exemplary 21st-century organization.

First, Brown is not in an information industry. His corporation, EBC Industries, Inc., formerly Erie Bolt Company, makes nuts and bolts—literally. Second, instead of trying to stamp out or buy out his competitors, he regularly partners with them. And finally, he mentors them. They remain independent and so does he.

"I've figured it out," Brown says. "I woke up at 4 o'clock this morning and finally figured out why we're different. Most companies focus on the competition, how to beat the competition. We focus on the customer, how to meet the customer's needs."

This simple shift enabled Brown to take off the typical business blinders. With his enthusiasm and energy, he has transformed a failing

Rust Belt business with 46 employees—with barely $3 million in revenues, losing at least $100,000 a year, and about six months from bankruptcy—into a thriving enterprise with 100 employees and revenues of $8 million. Note also this fact: he started this turnaround just before the 1987 stock market crash, that is, exactly when the U.S. economy fell into recession.

Brown and his cooperating competitors are very successful at what they do and very hard-working. Their success is based upon:

- A common business purpose: profit that comes from serving customers' needs.
- Some 20 or so allies, each with its independent specialty.
- Intense communication across and within company lines. People meet, fax, phone, and visit.
- Many leaders; leadership shifts, depending on the task at hand.
- Participation at all levels of all companies.

"I started doing this because it was common sense," Brown says simply. "If times weren't tough, I probably wouldn't have thought of it. But when things aren't going well, you're willing to try anything."

It all began when a customer asked Brown for something he didn't have. "A customer's order required secondary machining operations that we didn't have in-house," Brown explains. "So I called up a competitor, Joe Fedorko, at Diversified Manufacturing Company, who did, and it worked."

It worked so well that the next time Brown got an order he couldn't fill, he approached another competitor to whom he'd subcontracted in the past. "We found that they enjoyed doing business with us because there were no surprises. We shared process information, which reduced the number of rejects and streamlined production flow," says Brown. "This grew our product base, and we all started growing together."

Indeed, today, Brown's idea has grown into a thriving network that operates as a virtual factory complex—including competing specialty plating and coating companies, heat treaters, and machine shops.

APPLYING COMMON SENSE

There is nothing arcane about how Brown and his network do it.

"When we get a blueprint, we get together to discuss the best way to meet those requirements," Brown explains. "As soon as we arrive at the proper manufacturing process, we discuss costs to make sure we're competitive. Then we submit the bid."

They realize a 30 percent cost saving by using each other's capabilities, an advantage that they pass on to customers in lower prices and to themselves in reduced manufacturing expenses. Remarkably, each company in the network has more than doubled its business.

There are challenges, however, to regarding one another as virtual extensions of their own plants. It means that they share manufacturing process information, something most competitors fear. "There's always the potential that one of the companies might try to take on the business themselves," Brown says. "This happened once, but in the end, they lost the business because they didn't have the strength of the network. Word spread pretty rapidly, and it was difficult for them to create the relationships they needed to fulfill the contract. Violation of trust never works."

People from the other companies also walk in and out of one another's shops, a practice virtually unheard of in the highly competitive manufacturing world. They can spot new business opportunities and improve their processes as they learn about one another's operations.

For example, Brown's company produced a computer numerically controlled (CNC) machine part. "One of the companies in the network did not have the CNC software they needed to do the process efficiently," Brown recalls. "So we gave them our program, they modified it to fit their machine, and they did the operation more efficiently."

Although the teamnet members sometimes compete for the same business, they think the gains of sharing information far outweigh the risks of revealing trade secrets, Brown says.

Even the unions are on board. EBC Industries was the first company in the United Steel Workers to sign a five-year contract that includes provisions for flexible work schedules, in-house technical training, cross-training on three pieces of equipment, and profit sharing. "Pay levels increase as people gain additional technical expertise," Brown reports.

In 1990, EBC received the Pennsylvania Governor's Labor–Management Cooperation Award. "The union doesn't have any problem with this approach. They see that while there are layoffs all over town in union shops, we're hiring. Management and labor are working together to make sure jobs are more permanent than they were in the past."

It's a rather impressive story taken as a whole—a nuts-and-bolts company cooperating with its competitors that gets along with the union. EBC Industries' network shares five key principles with other teamnet organizations.

FIVE TEAMNET PRINCIPLES

You don't have to change everything to move into the Age of the Network. Harry Brown has created a teamnet with his competitors that offers their Industrial Age product in an Information Age style of business.

Brown successfully and aggressively engages in *co-opetition*: he cooperates with his competitors for business that he cannot do alone.

Let's look closely at the EBC strategy and note its five distinguishing features:

> • *Unifying Purpose*
> *Shared commitment to the same goal, not legalisms, holds the firms together.*

When asked the purpose of his network, Brown simply says, "profit." He also talks constantly about delighting his customers. He knows why he formed the network. Initially, it was for survival; then it proved to be very good for business.

> • *Independent Members*
> *Each company is different. Each retains its independence while cooperating with others on specific projects.*

Brown quickly reeled off the names of nine firms when asked to list the companies in his network—from the five-person contract machine shop, D&E Manufacturing, to the 130-person Erie Plating Company, which does special plating that meets stringent government specifications. Later that day, he faxed us a list of 12 additional companies, with names like American Tinning and Galvanizing, Hytech Metals, and Machining Concepts. There is no formal, set-in-stone membership—including about a dozen firms involved from the early days—and each company is completely independent, while being interdependent with the others.

> • *Voluntary Links*
> *They communicate extensively and meet often. No one is forced to participate. There are many crisscrossing relationships.*

"There are no regular meetings. No one wants them except on an as-needed basis to address problems as they surface," Brown says.

"Then we involve whoever's working on the project. We meet right on the shop floor. We have dry chalk boards by the machines so people can make notes as they go along. People know each other well. We fax a lot. We've experimented with e-mail, but mostly what we look at is graphics, so faxing is easier. Social get-togethers just happen—nothing formal."

Almost as an afterthought, he says, "We had some golf outings."

• *Multiple Leaders*
Different people and companies lead,
depending on what needs to be done. During
any given process, more than one person
leads.

"It's not so much product driven as process driven, so this happens automatically," Brown explains. "On one project, Champion Bolt [an Erie distributor and small-scale manufacturer of fasteners] had the initial lead in specifying the parts.

"Then we were working on some very difficult stainless steel material. We don't know that technology, so a vendor in our manufacturing group, Ron Wasielewski, who is a technical specialist in the latest cutting tools at Erie Industrial Supply, led that discussion. Now we're all at a higher level of knowledge."

Next, Russ Mollo, Brown's chief engineer, jumped back in when it came to heat treating. So it goes, with leaders changing over time.

"Russ is our resident agent of change and constant reminder to pull in all available resources to advance technologically and personally," Brown says. "Traditional job functions are gradually disappearing. As time goes on, there will be no defined engineering department, no defined sales department. The new organization will be a blend of various functions, resulting in streamlined communications and a more responsive source for our customers."[1]

- *Integrated Levels*
  *People work at many levels within EBC and
  within other partner companies in the
  teamnet that itself is part of the nuts-and-
  bolts business, which is embedded in the Erie
  County economy, which contributes to the
  U.S. industrial base.*

The owners of the firms, the hierarchy, are not the only ones who work together; the "lower-archy" does too. "Machine operators talk directly to one another. It may be rare in other shops but it's common practice here," Brown says. Communication is direct and doesn't have to go through approved channels.

Brown hesitates for a moment when asked to name the departments within his own company. "Well, let's see. The departments kind of bleed into each other." He mentions marketing and sales first, describing Vice President Norm Strandwitz as a "great advocate of team play and information sharing so that more information surfaces. He spends a lot of time on the shop floor."

Then Brown stops to think again, and says, "When you get past marketing, right around that same level, I'd put our QC [quality control] manager, Dan Neal." Brown goes on to describe the rest of the organization, including Joe Legnasky, who is the purchasing manager; Lew Vespoli, the treasurer, who "gets out on the shop floor"; Bob Valimont, the manufacturing manager, "who puts up with people strolling in and out of the shop"; right down to "the foreman in the forge shop and the hourly work force with group leaders."

Obviously, Brown isn't an executive who spends his days carefully designing and studying his organization chart. He just lives it.

Brown also sets his shop in a larger context, beginning with the Greater Erie area. "Any Rust Belt community has to look at what's happened to their business in the past and change," he says. "Then we are part of the nation's manufacturing base to compete globally. We have to pool our management skills so we can learn about our technology needs and assist one another."

A PATTERN LANGUAGE FOR ORGANIZING

The word "network" evokes a clear, simple mental model, a structure of points or circles and connecting lines—nodes and links, vibrant with activity. People intuitively use the idea with a remarkable consistency that continues to surprise us. Where people do get fuzzy is in describing how a network actually does anything coherent.

You probably already practice many of these principles. By simply upgrading your informal network knowledge and translating experience into a concise language, you will enhance your capabilities immediately. In the longer term, if you work with the principles and they work for you, you will gain the keys to networking, with its nearly universal applicability.

We began our search for principles when we started our research in 1979, and it continues today. Experience, examples, and thinking have led us to these five principles.

Purpose
Members
Links
Leaders
Levels

This set of patterns is not sacred. However, we have reviewed, tested, and seen them practiced extensively in every sector—business, nonprofit, grass-roots, government, religious, education—and in networks of all sizes.

Indeed, the great advantage of such timeworn general principles is their enormous power of applicability. Principles allow you to take knowledge from one situation and transfer it to another. People use principles at every level to design human-scale networks to meet their needs, while combining into ever-larger associations that reflect the same elements and dynamics.

Networks scale. No matter how exalted our role—royalty, board chair, or president—we all live in small groups. Small groups of people represent the largest organizations, embody corporations, and stand for the interests of entire industries. Little organizations make up big organizations. Everyone comes home at night to a small group, if only an extended one. Each of us plays many roles at many levels in many different groups.

What roles do you play at what levels? Seeing how you fit into your own picture is the first step in understanding the networks around you.

Apply the principles to the group closest to you personally and begin simply. Experiment with your own small group at work. Hold an informal planning session with a few close colleagues to try out the new ideas. Try the pocket tool outside of work: help a local school, church, temple, or community group form a network.

Through experience, you become a more astute observer of the organizational landscape. You learn by noticing what's happening in other companies. You recognize common features in the way nonbusiness organizations are coping with the transition from industry to information. See how others:

- Translate vision into work;
- Develop independent work units;
- Establish rich connections;
- Encourage multiple leaders; and
- Involve the hierarchy.

Suddenly, you become aware of things you haven't seen before— like the article in your trade publication about how a group of companies like yours is talking about forming an alliance that expands capabilities and enlarges the customer base. Perhaps you can join, or form the nucleus for a new network.

Now turn your thinking to teamnets and apply the principles to your own situation.

A POCKET TOOL FOR TEAMNETS

Consider the Five Teamnet Principles together as a mental tool, a Swiss Army pocket knife of the mind. Each principle is a separate tool that you can pull out and apply to your situation. They address different aspects of networks, but together they capture the integrated elements of a whole. "Doing it right" means using each principle appropriately, in the proper measure. When you succeed, you have a healthy teamnet.

THE PURPOSE OF PURPOSE

---

1. Purpose is the glue and the driver.

Every teamnet needs a clear purpose: "Win the MD-12 [Douglas Aircraft's still-on-the-drawing-board, next-generation wide-body,

POCKET TOOL OF TEAMNET PRINCIPLES

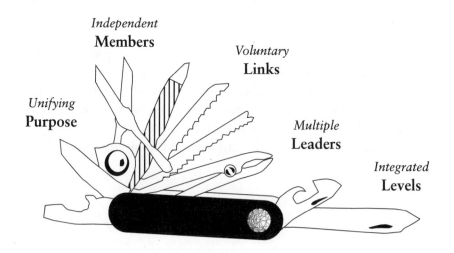

long-haul jumbo jet] systems integration contract and prepare our company to deliver it," says the computer company bid team. "Implement the new schedule planning process by 1 June," says the airline. "Cut operating costs by 20 percent in 60 days," says the hotel chain.

Teamnets achieve success by clearly defining their purpose. It needs to be simple, and everyone involved needs to understand it and, if possible, participate in its development. Each project in Harry Brown's manufacturing network has its clear purpose that derives from its overall one—meeting customers' needs and making a profit.

Purpose must extend from the abstract to the concrete to be truly useful. It begins with the organization's long-term vision, values, and strategy. These abstractions must translate into time-bound operational missions, measurable goals, clearly identifiable results, and, finally, specific tasks. Action must accompany beliefs and commitments, or the circuit never closes.

Purpose plays an absolutely critical role in teamnets. It establishes legitimacy, functioning in the place of the hire-fire power of hierarchy and the rules and regulations of bureaucracy. It is the basis for the agreements and voluntary relationships that constitute the "work life" of the network.

Which is not to say that purpose isn't important to other forms of organization. "What you're talking about are the Nine Principles of War," said Karl Leatham, a retired army lieutenant colonel, now a business process reengineering expert at Computer Sciences Corporation. "Just substitute the word 'competition' for 'enemy' and 'purpose' for 'target,' and you'll see what I mean." First among the Nine Principles is "The Objective: Direct every military operation toward a clearly defined, decisive, and attainable objective."[2]

Failure is easier to predict than success. A range with extremes can express each of the principles. We portray these extremes as "warnings" because they function as failure detectors. So, problems with purpose can range from too little to too much. Keep in mind that each is not the opposite but the complement of the other extreme. When one tendency threatens the health of a network, you need to introduce a dose of the other.

Warnings: From Glueless to Groupthink

Networks fail without enough purpose—"enough" being an impre-cise quantity that always depends on local circumstances and timing. Mostly, people know a motivating purpose when they both feel its power and understand its compelling logic. Teamnets, however, can easily fall apart after they form when the spark of purposeful life flickers and dies. Purpose is a vital source of energy that needs regular renewal, more often the more things change.

The more obscure extreme source of failure is "too much" purpose. "Groupthink" can also kill a network. People can lose their critical faculties when they become cohesive to the point of being cultlike. Purpose turns into ideology as the group discourages critical thinking. People make expensive mistakes when they put blinders on and refuse to tolerate divergent ideas. The need for diversity around purpose underlies the importance of independent members.

DECLARATION OF INDEPENDENCE

---

2. Each member has a healthy independence.

Think of it as a key test: You are not in a network if joining means you have to give up your independence. Members of networks—individuals in self-directed teams, departments cooperating in cross-functional programs, firms in alliance—retain and usually enhance their independence.

The parts of traditional organizations are dependent on a central and higher authority. Each company in Harry Brown's network stands on its own. Each will continue to exist even if the network collapses.

This principle underlies the virtual business known as VISA International. Financial institutions totalling 23,000 create its products, accepted by 11 million merchants in 250 countries and territories, whose data centers clear more transactions in one week than the

Federal Reserve system does in a year. Sales now equal the combined revenues of General Motors and IBM, having grown 20–50 percent, compounded annually, since VISA's birth in 1970. Dee Hock, founder and CEO emeritus of VISA International and VISA USA, established the business on simple principles, many of which stress the independence of its members:

- Equitable ownership by all participants;
- Maximum distribution of power and function;
- Distributed authority within each governing entity; and
- Infinitely malleable yet extremely durable.[3]

Consider, by analogy, the epochal change in the nature of computing in the last decade. Engineers designed computer systems in "master–slave" arrangements for most of their first 40 years: a glass-enclosed host computer with "dumb" dependent terminals attached. The entire system crashed when the central unit went down.

The unquestioned hegemony of huge mainframes in the Information Age was first shaken by the computer on a chip in the mid-1970s, which led to the personal computers (PCs) that decimated the centralized behemoths. The architecture of *networks* is ascendant in computing in the 1990s. PCs, workstations, mainframes, and other intelligent devices represent the independence of members connected in networks.

Members of a network are so substantial in their self-sufficiency that they do not depend on the network itself. A healthy independence is a necessity, even a prerequisite, for healthy interdependence.

Warnings: From Dependent to Stubborn

Networks fail at one extreme when their participants—whether organizations or individuals—cannot behave independently, the source of many network failures in large bureaucratic cultures. Bureaucrats may be free in theory, but in practice they fear making decisions and prevent others from taking responsibility that constitutes real independence. If you want a more flexible organization, be prepared not only to tolerate but to vigorously support risk taking.

People also carry independence to the other extreme, to stubborn-ness, where their narrow-minded behavior overwhelms cooperative efforts. Those who are so independent that they can't see a common purpose fragment the network, destroy its coherence, and doom it to fail. Small business networks often fail because some members are too stubbornly independent.

LINK CITY, PLANET EARTH

---

3. Teamnets have many links—expansive relationships among people and extensive connections through technology.

Many people wrongly regard a network as nothing more than a mesh of physical links. Even so, they unconsciously point to the network's distinguishing feature. Links—multifaceted, omnidirec-tional, complex, technical, and personal—are the cardinal charac-teristic of the Information Age organization.

First, see your links as the physical communication systems, besides meetings and collocation, that you use (or soon will): phones, faxes, memos, letters, overnight mail, conferencing (phone, video, computer), e-mail, the Internet, cellular phones, and mobile computing. The list goes on, and these are only the person-to-person media.

It's not news that our world is more connected than ever before and that the trend is accelerating. However, people misunderstand when they think that networks mean only computers, telephones, and other channels of communication.

Even technology networks are more than computers and tele-phones. What use is an e-mail or voice mail system if *people* aren't using it? Cayman Systems, a network hardware vendor, advertises that it "hasn't forgotten that what we're really connecting is people, not just computers."[4]

People develop relationships over time through their interactions. They must use physical links to communicate—channels to interactions to relationships and back.

Technology alone is inert. Look at the interactions that arise from the work to see a network in process, the pattern of who talks to whom how often. There trust develops and relationships crystallize— in the interactions over time and in moments of crisis. One company that installed a new communications system without a clue about how to use it to achieve more productive work relationships is representative of many that ignore the social side of change. New communication technologies stimulate new forms of organization and induce change, planned or not, desired or not.

Warnings: From Isolation to Overload

A lack of links is a clear cause of network failure. Missing physical connections, interactions that peter out, and stillborn relationships plague every network. No true network will form where personal connections are weak, that is, where people are not close. There is no trust without real relationships, and without trust, there is no network.

The failures caused by too many links, too many messages, and too quick a pace are less obvious. Overload is a major and widespread problem of the Information Age. You're in trouble when you dread calling into your voice mail or checking your e-mail because you know that once you begin, you're committed for the next few hours. Clogged communications systems shoot overload to first place on the failure indicator list for fast-growing networks. Overload depresses learning, which is central to the Information Age organization. The well-functioning teamnet manages information dynamically— filtering, categorizing, storing, sharing, and updating it, offering interpretation just in time—without great hassle.

CLIMBING THROUGH THE TEAMNET VINES

---

4. Fewer bosses, more leaders.

Everyone is a leader at the time when his or her unique experience and knowledge add to the group's intelligence. Bell Atlantic's CEO, Raymond W. Smith, describes leadership on "ever-shifting, cross-disciplinary teams" as "determined by who's most expert on the matter—not the corporate hierarchy."[5] That networks have multiple leaders surprises many people.

All human organizations have leaders—whether informal or formal. Hierarchy and bureaucracy minimize leadership; teamnets maximize it.

When Hyatt Hotels' sales and marketing organization went from functions to market segments, they appointed two leaders for each new market team. Each person holds a separate portfolio of responsibilities within the team. Everyone has something vital to contribute, with leadership broadly distributed.

Consider these questions to gauge whether you have fewer bosses and more leaders: Do you hear only one voice at meetings? Are there subgroups with task leaders? Does more than one person make commitments and take responsibility? Do people feel heard and believe that they have a voice in decision making? Do they participate—or at least feel that they can? This sense of participation is a key indicator of teamnet health.

Look for new styles of leadership. In particular, look for the natural networkers, the coordinators. These are the people at the nexus of relationships, people who are natural catalysts. They constantly develop matches between people's needs and resources.

Warnings: From Leaderless to Followerless

Without many leaders, networks fail, so it is easy to see how this spread-out organization could suffer from a lack of leadership. The "leaderless network" problem often creeps up slowly, almost undetected, as the original crop of leaders burns out before new leaders are ready to come online. Suddenly, one day the energy is gone, and no one knows why.

An abundance of leaders can bring its own problems. The "*prima donna* effect" is a good name for this extreme. Experts come in, do their work, and leave, while bosses breeze by, dropping orders, and special interests focus on their own niches. If we're all leaders but none of us has learned to follow, we have a power struggle on our hands. Incessant squabbles paralyze the network. Leading and following is a dance; step on as few toes as possible, please. Heed the motto that Hyatt Hotels put on its T-shirts: "Teamnet: It's an attitude."

THE HIERARCHY AND THE LOWER-ARCHY

---

5. Teamnets are naturally clumpy and clustered.

Contrary to popular belief, a network is not two-dimensional. Small groups, forming and re-forming, make up big networks. Even the smallest networks carry out work in subgroups of ones, twos, or threes.

The word "teamnet" carries connotations of this multilevel reality: networks of teams of people.

Groups within groups nest internally in some teamnets. Arthur Andersen & Co.'s Business Systems Consulting group (BSC), headquartered in Boston, comprises 765 consultants spread throughout the world in 80 locations housing 2 to 45 people, each helping small to medium-sized businesses install technology networks to meet business needs. The teams are local; the network is global. BSC, in turn, is part of Arthur Andersen's Audit and Business Advisory Services group, which reports to the managing partner–CEO of Arthur Andersen & Company, S.C., the main partnership that holds both Arthur Andersen and Andersen Consulting.

Externally, teamnets are open organizations that evolve along with their environments. So it is equally important to consider the larger context. Teamnets may be part of a larger enterprise or part of an industry, market, or movement—a hierarchy of levels.

We tend to network at our own level, where it is easiest to establish peer relationships, ignoring the other levels at our peril.

Warnings: From No Uplinks to No Downlinks

It's easy to lose touch with the hierarchy, but it's very dangerous. Many a promising teamnet effort has succeeded briefly, then shriveled and died because it lacked links to the senior levels of the company or to the stakeholder opinion leaders. In one dramatic case involving two companies, the vendor's executive committee killed a huge deal at the last minute because it was not briefed on the project until the moment of final decision. Often, problems with the hierarchy show up late in a change process rather than earlier, when there is still time to address them. Remember: the hierarchy always has the last word.

It is just as dangerous to forget the ground floor, where work takes place, the people at the operating levels who support the network's activities. The people on the front lines of production, such as Harry Brown's hourly work force in Erie, Pennsylvania, and those in services, such as at the front desk of the Marriott in Jacksonville, Florida, need to network. Customers and suppliers need involvement up and down the line rather than simply as passive recipients in a situation where only a salesperson and a purchaser communicate. Change is killed just as effectively from below as from above. When people on the front line are out of touch, they shield themselves from innovations launched from above, which causes unintended side effects.

UP THE ORGANIZATIONAL SCALE

New organizations are erupting at every level—from very small groups to global networks. Companies are furiously experimenting and learning, creating a profusion and confusion of management innovations. It's all happening at the boundary between the Industrial and Information ages.

A massive shift has been underway for half a century. From its zenith, the Industrial Age descends while the Information Age ascends. Decade by decade, the pace of change has been picking up.

While they work an honored spirit, some "new" ideas simply fix what appears to be broken. They are like the people who drew ever more complex epicycles to make Ptolemy's predictions work in spite of new astronomical data that completely refuted the Ptolemaic universe. Some people only look backward as the end of an age challenges their power. Sometimes their solutions are very elaborate and work well—for a while.

Other "new" ideas are different, stimulated by authentic changes. Their goal is to fit form to new, constantly changing functions. They have many names, but all share a common set of network characteristics reflected in the Five Teamnet Principles. Networked organizations can comprise hierarchies and bureaucracies, or function within them with infinite variations.

Safeguard Scientifics, Inc., a networking partnership of companies, that work together turns this idea into strategy. "In the challenging business environment of the next decade, the ability to network effectively, both within the corporate organization and externally with other companies, will be a key strategic element to increased competitiveness and greater productivity," says the company's annual report.[6]

Teamnets appear all along the organizational scale—from very small internal units to macroeconomic groups that interest nations.[7]

TEAMNETS ALONG THE ORGANIZATIONAL SCALE

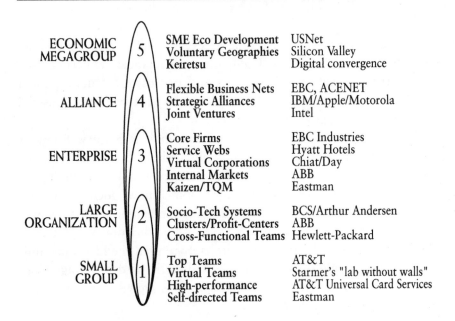

ECONOMIC MEGAGROUP	5	SME Eco Development Voluntary Geographies Keiretsu	USNet Silicon Valley Digital convergence
ALLIANCE	4	Flexible Business Nets Strategic Alliances Joint Ventures	EBC, ACENET IBM/Apple/Motorola Intel
ENTERPRISE	3	Core Firms Service Webs Virtual Corporations Internal Markets Kaizen/TQM	EBC Industries Hyatt Hotels Chiat/Day ABB Eastman
LARGE ORGANIZATION	2	Socio-Tech Systems Clusters/Profit-Centers Cross-Functional Teams	BCS/Arthur Andersen ABB Hewlett-Packard
SMALL GROUP	1	Top Teams Virtual Teams High-performance Self-directed Teams	AT&T Starmer's "lab without walls" AT&T Universal Card Services Eastman

THE LARGE LIFE OF THE SMALL GROUP

Many small groups, but not all, have teamnet characteristics. The academic discipline of "social network analysis" studies life's informal small groups and extended networks of associations, the "sea of social relationships" in which we all are embedded. Business is both awash in informal networks of small groups and replete with hierarchical and bureaucratic small groups that run solely by commands, controls, and procedures. Usually these are formal organizational units with standard operating procedures.

Increasingly, however, networked small groups are appearing as part of the formal management structure. Small, goal-oriented, peer-based, richly linked, multileadered *teams* are the most common prescription for leading-edge management in the 21st century.

Procter & Gamble has been using *self-directed teams* since the 1960s; Cummins Engine began experimenting in the 1970s. Saturn is

General Motors's company-within-a-company that built a culture of empowered teams and lean hierarchy from day one. Eastman Chemical Company uses a self-directed team to run its senior manufacturing management function, as well as hundreds of others at all levels.

High-performance teams call out the best in people as they combine innovative management approaches with information technologies. In these efforts, careful attention to how teamnet principles affect both people and technology reaps great rewards. AT&T Universal Card Services has developed an approach called "loose-tight": loose guidelines for a team empowered to take action, with a tight focus on goals and results.

Virtual small teams span the globe for the electronically enabled, like those in computer scientist/cardiologist Frank Starmer's "lab without walls." These new kinds of instantly interacting but physically distributed groups are both formal and informal. One of Bell Northern's R&D labs extends from several sites in North America to several in China; each Monday morning, Ottawa time, all dozen members participate in a conference call. Hints of the power of the new media to spawn informal social networks appear everywhere—from the news groups and chat channels of the Internet to the burgeoning commercial services like America Online to the countless bulletin boards catering to every need and locality.

Teams exist at all levels, from top to bottom. Where there is change, teams are often not far behind. ABB's functional units are fading as people organize into "Target-Oriented Teams," emphasizing their purpose. Sixteen TOTs exist among 200 employees in one of ABB's Swedish companies. The TOTs are organized into profit centers, and the profit centers, in turn, are organized into companies. Small teams run what's left of the headquarters staff at the company and country levels of this $30 billion behemoth. Only five levels away from the TOTs sits CEO Percy Barnevik, who is part of an executive *top team* of 13 that meets every three weeks to set global strategy.

We asked Gösta Lundqvist, one of five change agents on the corporate staff that serves ABB's 100 Swedish companies, what happened to the specific functions, such as engineering, sales, and marketing. He waved his hand and said nonchalantly, "They just went away."

MAKING A LARGE ORGANIZATION SEEM SMALL

It is surprisingly easy to build temporary teamnets within and between bureaucracies. Most companies today routinely form *cross-functional teams*, whether they call them that or not. Here the purpose is palpable and the need to cooperate across boundaries for the good of the whole is clear. Departments, functional groups, or agencies send representatives, draw up charters, and appoint a leader. The team segments its work through task leaders and proceeds, often with breathless speed, until it accomplishes its mission. Then it disbands.

These one-at-a-time anomalies are true teamnets—and great learning environments. The challenge, however, is to fully realize the power of cross-boundary work internally. Toyota Motor Company is world renowned for its ability to plan and manage horizontal relationships and processes across all functions. Hewlett-Packard, an acknowledged U.S. leader, set up companywide "councils" of cross-functional efforts that are themselves coordinated through a Product Generation Process Council.

Many companies find that there is a "natural size" for self-reliant organizational units. W.L. Gore & Associates, the $1 billion maker of Gore-Tex, regards 150–200 people as a roughly optimal size for the manufacturing facilities that populate their "lattice organization." Parts of British Petroleum and General Electric Canada form *cluster organizations*, units large enough to maintain their own administrative apparatus and small enough to be responsive to customers. D. Quinn Mills's research suggests that 30–50 people is an effective size range for these units.[8]

Stories of pioneering, derring-do megaprojects carried out at the speed of light across continents reach back only a few years. One example is Digital Equipment Corporation's globally distributed teamnet in the late 1980s, code-named Calypso, that built its state-of-the-art midrange computer in record time, earning billions of dollars for the company. Once a bold new concept, *social-technical systems* reflects what is now a mainstream effort to relate organizational change to emerging technologies. The objective is to ensure greater freedom for the individual (social) while increasing collective productivity (technical).

THE ELEGANTLY NETWORKED ENTERPRISE

Teamnets appear in various guises at the whole-enterprise (company/corporate) level. Even small firms operate through smaller internal components. Enterprise teamnets are also the crossroads for a great variety of external relationships and partnerships.

Some enterprises, more than others, vividly demonstrate the network form as a whole, though all incorporated organizations are to some degree teamnets (e.g., connected components, multilevel, purpose-directed). Eastman Chemical Company is an example of a 21st-century quality organization that is succeeding today. It got there by practicing the Japanese principle of *kaizen*. *Kaizen*, literally "continuous improvement involving everyone,"[9] is a companywide, total quality management system that, when fully deployed, is a teamnet. Improvement involves every part of the company at all times.

The use of *internal markets* is one astonishingly creative way to bust bureaucracy and empower internally independent organizations. ABB, known for its extremely lean bureaucracies and flat hierarchies, is a world-class exemplar of this strategy. The principle is simple: any internal unit is free to buy and sell *externally* as well as *internally*. This practice eliminates a welter of internal rules, procedures, and transfer prices. It offers enormous autonomy within organizations and ensures that people throughout the enterprise experience market realities.

The advantage of internal markets, Gifford and Elizabeth Pinchot write, is that they take "decisions a bureaucracy would bungle" and turn "them over to the cutting intelligence of marketplace choice."[10] In the words of William Halal, management professor at George Washington University, "[I]nternal markets are replacing hierarchy."[11]

Virtual corporations[12] allow companies to radically alter their way of doing business without extensive new investment. For example, Chiat/Day, a leading advertising firm, joins its nine offices, using 700

Macintosh computers in the United States, Canada, and England, and clients and vendors, including their travel agent, with a sophisticated e-mail network. "[W]e intend . . . to become a virtual agency," said Steve Alburty, management information system director. "We're getting rid of all our desks. We'll be working from home or client sites, our office space will be shrunk to a third of its current size, and what's left will mostly be converted to meeting rooms."[13]

Some organizations, such as *service webs*, are distributed by their very nature—spread-out organizations composed of semi-autonomous units. Hyatt Hotels is a management company for more than 100 hotels, each with a separate set of owners and expectations. Professional service firms are spreading out as they hasten to adapt to the pace of change engulfing their businesses. Most of the Big 6 accounting firms and many consulting companies—already highly distributed corporate designs with local offices around the world and partnership power structures—have been reorganizing to include cross-boundary organizations (e.g., KPMG Peat Marwick's lines of business) and teams to serve market segments and customers.

Finally, *core firms*, like EBC Industries, with both vendor and customer partnerships, are inventing new structures to enhance their competitiveness. Traditional core–supplier configurations have a giant core and small, isolated, scrambling suppliers, but in the EBC network, purpose and personal relationships identify the center. Connections go directly from member to member, node to node, not necessarily through the core. Big companies like Chrysler are doing the same thing. "Chrysler and its suppliers are a virtual enterprise," President Robert A. Lutz told *The Wall Street Journal*.[14]

ALLIANCES, NOT MERGERS, THANKS

Links among companies proliferate as business speeds up and goes global. *Joint ventures* are a traditional form of partnership, a minimal network, in which two or more companies form a separate corporate entity that they jointly own. The most successful such ventures, such as the 60 or so created by Corning, Inc., reflect all five teamnet principles: clear purposes; independence not only among the partners but also of the created company; rich relationships to exploit the complementary capabilities of each party; multiple leaders (at least three sets); and many levels and boundaries to climb over and through in all the interacting enterprises.

Intel, the microprocessor manufacturer, is generating most of its new business in joint ventures: with Microsoft to create a telephone linking standard; with Microsoft and General Instrument to build an interactive TV-top cable converter; and with, among others, Bell-South, Bell Atlantic, Ameritech, Siemens, and Alcatel.[15]

The dominant business phenomenon of the 1990s is networking, a much more flexible and fluid mode than its predecessors. It contrasts with the merger mania of the 1980s and the traditional industrial response of gobbling up the competition and getting bigger. We are witnessing an explosion of new, large-scale, multicorporate networks that offer both cooperation and competition in a veritable zoo of *strategic alliances*. Such alliances are true networks in which the independence of members is as clear and unquestioned as the inappropriateness of hierarchy. With the independence of members and multiple leadership as basic premises, the trick lies in creative development of joint purposes and voluntary relationships.

Two-party alliances are still the norm, but multimember alliances are becoming increasingly common. Small businesses are also engaging in this fast-growing trend to ally in a big way. *Flexible business networks* are taking hold throughout the world, including in the United States, some stimulated by government funds, countless others started by the companies themselves.[16] These small company alliances offer a remarkable demonstration of the economic value of business links among independent companies.

BEYOND ALLIANCES: MEGAGROUPS

Beyond the reach of individual firms are massive conglomerations of economic activity that are to some degree integrated and focused. These very-large-scale entities are likely to acquire increasing

importance in the future. Known in Japan as *keiretsu*, they are link-
ages among a large number of firms in diverse industries anchored by
a major bank or manufacturer. Massive webs of strategic alliances are
now appearing elsewhere on the global stage. Global "digital
keiretsu"—the 18 companies that swirl around Toshiba, for
example[17]—are shaping the future convergence of computers, tele-
communications, and media.

AnnaLee Saxenian's study of the contrasting fates of Route 128 in
Massachusetts and Silicon Valley in California underscores the enormous importance of a regional business culture conducive to the
formation of networks. These *voluntary geographies* are gaining
ground as people take a more consciously regional and ecological
view of their businesses.

Small and medium-sized enterprise economic development, based
on thousands of flexible business networks, is one of the most promising approaches for improving our myriad engines of job growth.
USNet, a private, nonprofit initiative funded through defense conver-
sion grant money and state matching grants, provides services to a
consortium of 15 states that encourage these networks.

In short, teamnets surface at all levels of organizations. While some
networks demonstrate the five teamnet principles better than others,
all reflect the principles to some degree. They are changing businesses
and organizations of all sizes everywhere.

CHAPTER 5

RX FOR MONDAY MORNING: TURNING PRINCIPLES INTO PRACTICE

LIFE-LONG LEARNING

Asea Brown Boveri (ABB) is an excellent example of a sets-within-sets-within-sets corporate organization: it has 1,300 separate companies employing 250,000 people in 100 countries who generate $30 billion in annual revenues.

At ABB Network Control AB, one of 100 ABB firms in Sweden that comprise ABB CEWE, Thommy Haglund had the task of implementing a "learning organization" pilot in the 300-person, white-collar software company, where half of the employees have college degrees. In the rapidly changing world of software, ongoing learning is critical. The company already had decentralized its functions and flattened its hierarchy (from six levels to three and from 40 managers to 20), and it was ready to move forward.

The first thing they did was to throw out the term "learning organization" and replace it with what became known as "3L," standing for "Life-Long Learning." "This is very personal," Haglund explained, pointing to the need for each person in the organization to be a life-long learner.

Many ABB employees were not learners, much less life-long ones, when they began. They typified the problem by poking fun at themselves and inventing a mythical employee with low self-esteem.

105

Sigurd's uncommon Swedish name implied that he was somewhat "out of it." His dejected, slightly disheveled cartoon image matched his character: he thought he couldn't influence his situation; he didn't understand how his organization worked; he had no plan for developing his competencies; and he thought (when he did so) that his manager was responsible for his education.

"We were running beside the bike," Haglund explained, "and there were lots of excuses going around. As one person said, 'When you point your finger, there are three fingers pointing back at you.' "

So they set up 20 "Idea Groups" of 15 people each, whose task was to have creative conversations. The Idea Groups, selected for a maximum mix of cross-functional men and women, younger and older people who were strangers to one another in the organization, involved no management. Getting new people acquainted with one another was an implicit goal.

"We gave them some easy questions that had very hard answers," Haglund said:

- What is competence?
- What is competence development?
- What needs exist?
- Who is responsible?
- What can I do immediately?
- What have we learned from this?

Everyone kept a diary and was asked to write two or three sentences each day for a week in answer to the question "What have I learned?"

It was, Haglund says, "six months of storming. We had to keep reminding ourselves that it has to look bad before it looks better. But you can't shortcut that period."

It also was not free. Each Idea Group received $5,000 (for an overall investment of $100,000 for the 20 groups), but with strings attached. "They couldn't spend it on training, they couldn't split it up, that is, they had to spend it together, and they had to spend it in three months."

The program was a resounding success. The "Idea" Groups came up with all sorts of new concepts. Creativity ran rampant, turning traditional approaches into home-grown, innovative ones. A course in presentation skills became an amateur theater presentation. Survival expeditions replaced courses in teamwork. Instead of setting up a huge administrative system to book everything, they used a bulletin board.

Today internal seminars take place regularly, with such titles as "Lateral Thinking" and "Technical Training for Nontechies." At the same time:

- Mentors have become common, including 26 internal people who took on mentees, while 40 others (about 15 percent of the employees) gained mentors in other ABB companies.
- Interns now cross internal boundaries by spending a week in another department.
- Intercompany visits are common and encouraged.
- Development people regularly visit customers, a practice previously unheard of.

Eighteen months into the three-year pilot program, they like their results. Company revenues have grown. We asked Haglund what will happen when the program ends. "I want to try something else," he replied smiling.

TAKING THE FIRST STEPS

You do not have to scrap your whole organization and begin anew to shift your business into the Age of the Network. Starting small, as ABB Network Control did with groups of 15, you can develop your teamnet over time.

Choose a project with a clear mission that involves people from more than one organization. In ABB's case, the mission—to become a learning organization—was quite grand. They introduced it modestly as a pilot program. To qualify for this approach, the project must cross at least a few traditional boundaries—organizational, corporate, or geographic.

Hold a briefing for the people involved in the project on the five principles described in the previous chapter—purpose, members, links, leaders, and levels. Then follow through with these two steps:

- *Startup:* Do an initial teamnet assessment.
- *Launch:* Hold a planning session when the teamnet is ready to take off.

With planning launched, you must implement. (In chapter 4, we laid out the warning signs that impede successful implementation.) Maintain a steady course throughout the project's life by keeping close watch on the dynamic extremes of each of the five principles. We focus particular attention on the startup and launch phases here because, without a successful start, the teamnet will never get to implementation.

Every project, every organization, grows over time; it is a process with a beginning, middle, and end. In each phase, use the Five Teamnet Principles to tune up your process.

STARTUP: ASSESSING THE SITUATION

This is your first quick pass at applying the principles, which you will plumb further in the launch phase.

Use the principles as a mental checklist for a set of conversations or a simple start. Ask people:

- Does everyone have a *common view* of the project?
- Do you consider yourselves *colleagues*?

- Do you have rich *connections* among you?
- Can you hear many *voices* within the group?
- Are you *inclusive* of the levels of organization?

This checklist provides a quick summary of how far along a group is on the teamnet path.

Common View?

Does everyone share a common view of the work? There is an easy way to test this. Separately, ask three members what the group's purpose is. Three quite different answers indicate that the focus is fuzzy at best. You are not necessarily home free, however, if everyone repeats the same mantra. This may suggest groupthink, the uncritical acceptance of a group ideology.

The answers you are looking for show strong common themes with unique twists and special applications. In healthy teamnets, people share deeper levels of vision, values, trust, and core beliefs while holding diverse viewpoints and arguing over individual issues.

Teamnets never really jell and cannot succeed without a shared purpose. A teamnet faces the clearest danger if it once had a purpose that is no longer clear. Rarely will it succeed by maintaining the organization in its current form. A purposeful organization that completes its work, delivers its results, and goes out of business is a graceful and natural course of a useful but transient teamnet.

To come to life, teams and networks need a purpose that everyone understands.

Colleagues?

Who is involved? Practically, this means "get names." Whether recorded on the back of an envelope or published in a directory, names of people and organizations that need representation indicate membership in the teamnet.

You gain early clues to the potential size and multiple levels of the teamnet by understanding who the members are and what talents they bring. These are the *part*-icipants, the components, the most tangible elements of the basic network.

Listen to how the participants talk about one another and the organizations they represent. Do they refer to and treat one another with respect, communicate as peers, and possess elements of independence? These are all nuances of the word "colleagues."

Quickly assess how independent, dependent, and interdependent the members are. Dependent members are a drag on the whole group; totally independent members rip it apart. Interdependence is a necessary balance.

Look for the obvious. Can participants stand on their own if the group as a whole fails?

Will companies remain independent in an alliance? Do individuals on a cross-functional team have a home organization and other responsibilities? Do physically distributed sites have control over their budgets? Does a line-of-business profit center also have personnel authority?

Connections?

Just because people regard one another as colleagues and share a vision does not mean they have a teamnet. The third *sine qua non* is links. There are no relationships without communication around joint activity, and without relationships among participants, there is no network.

Look for the "1–2–3" of the links. The channels (1) allow people to interact (2), which is how they form relationships (3).

1. *Look for the physical channels.*
2. *Identify the tangible interactions.*
3. *Recognize the relationships among people.*

First, in what ways does your group link now? People create links with all kinds of media—frequent face-to-face meetings, conferences, conventions, off-sites, phone calls, faxes, newsletters, video, e-mail, and a rapidly growing list of exotic electronic technologies. Only preferences, time, and money limit this cornucopia of connections.

Groups that work together across separate locations or in the same location but at different times, such as shifts of nurses, need to be explicit about communication. How do people communicate with one another? Are they clear and intentional, or vague or inconsistent about the channels they use?

Second, look for the interactions, the actual use people make of the group's communication systems. Get a feel for the levels of activity. A simple survey can yield dramatic findings. Do higher-ups respond to lower-downs, or do they ignore them? Do people talk only to others at their own level? Are the actions and reactions of senders and receivers sparse and distant? Or is there a buzzing, booming confusion, which is the profuse, immediate, and spontaneous stuff of real communication?

Third, rise up to the 30,000-foot view (see chapter 1), where you can see the whole communication pattern. Can you see the basic relationships, the standing waves of interaction over time? Are there broad streams of communication that indicate a history and a culture together? On a fast-moving team, bonds form quickly through intense interaction within a quickly clicking culture. If there are voids here, brainstorm ways to increase meaningful interactions.

Relationships can become real in an instant, or they may emerge slowly as a pattern of interaction establishes itself in response to change. This is true for people and for organizations. Regardless of time, relationships form the bonds that build trust. The teamnet goes nowhere without trust.

Voices?

Do you hear one or many voices when you listen to the group? Heard from the outside, one voice might sound like a coherent teamnet with a spokesperson. Now look inside. It's likely to be a hierarchy at heart if the same one voice drowns out the rest.

Ask a few people in the group who the leaders are. Listen for a plural response if you ask the question in the singular. Better yet, stand corrected as people talk about how important everyone's role is.

All groups, including teams and networks, have leaders. Teamnets, however, have more leaders than hierarchy and bureaucracy. Where a hierarchy insists on one leader, a network has several. Where a bureaucracy seeks terms of office for single leaders and appoints subordinate bosses, a network sees a number of leaders rotate through diverse responsibilities.

Is this healthy? The answer is no if fluid leadership indicates a fragmented, out-of-control group. The answer is yes if it indicates a dynamic capacity to self-organize continuously to meet changing conditions.

Whether many voices indicate useless babble or deep bonds depends on the purpose that unites them. Are the shifting leaders also keeping the group focused on the overall purpose? Are people stepping up to responsibilities as needed, then stepping aside as new expertise is required? In the end, is the purpose being accomplished?

Inclusive?

Finally, to put all this information together, you need to sort out the levels. What parts of the organization does the teamnet include and what is it included within? What is the overall context, the greater environment? What are its major internal components? What makes them up?

Inclusion works both ways, internally and externally. You include the participants when you take the point of view of the teamnet. When you take the point of view of the participants, the teamnet includes you.

It is essential to adopt various points of reference in the 21st-century organization. At minimum, people need to be able to understand the point of view of the organization as a whole, as well as the reference point of their part of it.

Though multiple points of view are free, they are like mountain tops, requiring effort to attain.

Once you see the levels, look for the relationships across them. Crossing boundaries often involves traversing levels from someone's point of view. In a world of wholes and parts, there is no other way.

Practically, this means people from diverse ranks working together. Are there ongoing connections with the hierarchy that your teamnet sits within? Are there links to the operating lower-archy? If your teamnet spans two companies, is the alliance simply a relationship at the top or the middle, or are there interactions at many levels among the allied organizations?

LAUNCH: PLANNING THE WORK

Teamnets need to be self-organizing to some extent to be successful. The more rapid the change and the more fluid the organization, the greater the need for this capacity.

The recipe for self-organization begins with people:

- *People create the shared purpose.* Whether a team working together at a white board, an omnipotent ruler issuing an edict, or a lawmaker writing a preamble, people are the ultimate source of an organization's *raison d'être.*

- *Purpose generates the work.* "Why" leads to "what." This is essential in networks because purpose is the source of legitimacy for activities undertaken and results achieved.
- *Cross-boundary work becomes explicit through planning.* People need maps to help guide work through unfamiliar geographic locations. Teams that work at a distance need to be more explicit than those in one location.
- *"Those who do, plan."* Participatory planning provides the energy for the self-organizing process. Openness and inclusion lead to trust. To maximize everyone's sense of involvement, invite everyone, expect some to show up, and profusely thank the few who stay to do the work.

Planning is a continuous process of thinking both about the long-range future and about what to do next. One pass at planning is never enough. A plan is never finished but is often "good enough for now."

All five Teamnet Principles interrelate. Change in one principle area effects the others. Use a draft purpose statement to broaden the circle of stakeholders, who in turn reshape the focus. Actual relationships will differ from those proposed and will lead to different leaders. More work leads to more internal units and more external alliances.

Set up a planning process that makes the work real, gains commitments, and kick-starts the internal leadership. Make the process as participatory as possible. In words attributed to General Dwight D. Eisenhower:

The plan is nothing. Planning is everything.[1]

Call a planning meeting and include these agenda items:

- Clarify purpose.
- Identify members.

- Establish links.
- Multiply leaders.
- Integrate levels.

These action statements also can guide a longer planning agenda stretching over days or months. For example, take the first item, "Clarify purpose." In some situations, a few minutes of discussion will reaffirm a common understanding; in others, extensive programs will be set in motion to discover a new vision and mission. Just getting to "Go" in a teamnet is often a considerable accomplishment.

Clarify Purpose

Purpose is the essential resource available to a teamnet. To make purpose useful, you need to "unpack it," that is, to translate values, vision, and mission into goals, tasks, and results.

When people are physically distributed, their purpose needs to go beyond the unspoken and tacit behavior that works for those who are near one another. People need to generate and interpret the purpose so that they understand it well enough to bring it back to their diverse locations and communicate it to other people. Internal direction cannot replace external command unless people participate in the process of defining their work. People can then carry the explicit purpose across boundaries.

If you have already gone through a period of searching and struggling to reach a new vision and *mission*, now is the time to translate the abstractions into concrete terms. Set your *goals* for the future—only a handful, please! Brainstorm many goals, but select only a few. The "rule of seven," the number of things people can comfortably keep in mind at once, is strongly applicable here.

Next, pick a time horizon—a week, a month, a year—and place yourself at this future point and look back. Ask what *results* you want to achieve within that time for each goal. Results are the output, the deliverables, the products of a group's activities. Finally, identify the *tasks* that connect the goals to the results.

CONVERTING PURPOSE INTO WORK

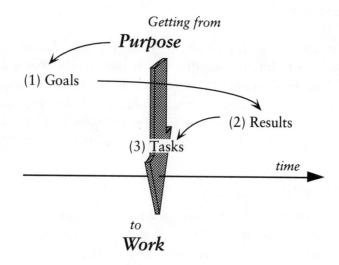

When you arrive at tasks this way, you have made the purpose concrete. People understand the legitimacy of the tasks since they can relate them directly to the overall shared purpose. And if the purpose changes, they know that the tasks need reevaluation.

Identify Members

Now that you know what the work is, who needs to participate in what? Here is one of the secrets of successful networking:

> *Everyone does not have to participate in everything.*

Each task, driven by a goal, has at least one result and represents a chunk of work carried out by a subgroup, a part of the teamnet. Only some members need to be involved in most tasks, perhaps as few as one or two. For certain tasks, such as a milestone review, everyone may need to participate. Members sign up by sharing the work through one or more of the group's activities. "Members" are the arms and legs and torso and senses of an organization. In teamnets, "they" becomes "we."

Membership goes beyond names on a list to flesh-and-blood commitments as the planning phase unfolds and the work is clarified. These groups define their boundaries by identifying their members.

A core group expands its network view to include stakeholders and constituencies beyond itself that need representation in the plans. Customers, for example, may participate as full, temporary, or *ex officio* members of a network.

Some teams and networks may have distinct boundaries, but often they are bounded from the center. Core members, perhaps identified directly as a set of individuals, sit at the center of intersecting relationships. Further out, organizational names or positional titles identify participants and stakeholders. Furthest out, people refer to constituencies by general categories, such as "customers," "media," and "government."

Don't be afraid to name members of a network at all these levels of abstraction at once. Networks include individuals and organizations. People may act for themselves, stand for a group, or represent a constituency—all at the same time.

Establish Links

We need to take our thinking up a level for a moment as the focus comes back to the links again. This is where the 21st-century organization is going to look especially different from its predecessors.

The convergence of digital technologies drives inescapable organizational change as the interconnected global network grows, along with individual information mobility. A few years from now, connectivity will explode dramatically. We put our bet on 2001 as the year when large-scale "digital convergence" snaps into place and an order-of-magnitude new jolt of change hits.

We are in the midst of epochal change in our ability to link. This is not only a technology revolution but a social one as well. The plummeting cost of connectivity itself challenges the vertical channels of hierarchical information flow. Distributed, plentiful information enables distributed power.

Think about links at two levels: first, for the group as a whole, and second, for specific tasks and subgroups. Indeed, you need to move through these perspectives several times to find a good mix of media.

You need to establish a communications environment for the group that supports its work and is conducive to growing relationships. Consider multiple means for the physical links. Different people prefer different media; some personal preferences are extremely strong. The nature of the work and the location of the people greatly influence the choice and mix of media. In particular, cross-boundary work virtually guarantees the need for more than one mode of communication.

The answers are not always obvious. While it might appear that fax is a preferable mode of communication because of its simplicity, in some places e-mail is preferable. "Fax is very hard for us," says Olya Marakova, a scientist in Frank Starmer's lab without walls doing basic research on cardiac cells, in an e-mail message from Pushchino, Russia. "We have only one fax machine for several buildings, and it's very expensive. But everyone has modems, and it takes no time to send e-mail."

Harry Brown's EBC Industries' teamnet, by contrast, depends heavily on fax because e-mail cannot easily transport the complex manufacturing drawings that the companies exchange. Not everyone has Marakova's fax deficiency or Brown's need, but they make the point that the communication mode depends on the situation.

Next, lay the groundwork for specific relationships to develop in planning a teamnet. You know that you want marketing people to work with their counterparts in finance. Here you work to relate (soft) relationships to (hard) technology in reverse of what you do in the assessment phase, where you begin with the technology and work to the relationships.

- The purpose is the source of a desire or need to establish relationships.
- By translating the purpose into concrete work activities, you describe the interactions that need to be supported.
- Choose and set up the physical channels of communication required by the interactions.

In short, work drives the technology, rather than the reverse.

Multiply Leaders

This is a teamnet commandment. It's also where some people have the most trouble with the teamnet idea—fearing either powerlessness or anarchy. "If you tell people they've going to have to give up power, they'll tell you to stuff it," says former Xerox CEO David Kearns.[2] "The risk of democracy" is how one besieged airline executive put it.

We never said it is easy, only that this is the way things are going to be. Potentially, this is the most personally powerful aspect of teamnets. There is more room and more need for people to take responsibility and exercise leadership because the group is working on many complex issues concurrently.

Most groups include both appointed and natural leaders. Cross-boundary groups need to include people with positional power. A teamnet is no different from a bureaucratic committee that studies and recommends if it has no power to act. Groups develop their own leaders, regardless of the official structure. In networks, people use this ability to great advantage.

Natural leadership in a group springs up around its activities. People take responsibility for particular tasks and in this way are self-organizing. You can use the work to define leadership within the group, rather than the other way around.

When people generate their own tasks, they see why they need to be involved in specific activities. They are able to add unique contributions, exercising leadership as they do, since they know their own expertise, experience, or perspective. Each person in the teamnet is a leader at some time in some activities.

Each cross-boundary task and set of activities offers an opportunity for leadership within the teamnet. Task leadership emerges as people take on responsibility for results. Linking specific results with specific people anchors responsibility for work.

Many tasks naturally lend themselves to coleaders, which further expands the possibilities for leaders. These leadership roles also naturally end as the work is completed and the process moves on.

What you *don't* want to do is what bureaucracy does—chunk all the work down to the level of individual tasks. This suppresses multiple leadership, proves more costly, and does not work in complex situations.

Integrate Levels

Purpose, members, links, and leaders all involve multiple levels of consideration. Teamnets are at least three levels deep: the members of the teams, the teams themselves, and the network of teams (or individuals in task groups in teams).

Don't be afraid to connect across the levels or even to confuse them. Levels *are* often confusing. Just keep moving your thinking up and down the scales of size and scope, looking internally and externally from the boundaries, from global to local perspectives and back again.

The planning process itself is one of the best means of integrating the levels and keeping everyone informed. Indeed, early plans are often most valuable as tools for communicating with the hierarchy. They are also great recruitment devices for potential participants not involved in the initial planning.

Can you fit your plan on a page? If so, you have a grasp of the whole that you can communicate to others. Can you break down the one-page plan to a greater level of detail, complete with places and dates? This indicates that your plan has depth. Can you fit your plan into a broader strategy and overall purpose? This indicates that your plan has a context, another way of integrating levels.

Use precious meeting resources to develop a clear, high-level picture that people can go away and fill in. Each person needs to understand the whole, and each leader needs to balance global issues with local concerns.

By ending the launch phase with a high-level picture, you have brought your original fuzzy, 30,000-foot view down to a sufficient level of detail to do some real work. This degree of clarity in the work convinces others that the plan makes sense, simplifying the "marketing" of the idea. Having taken the time to go to this level of detail, you now can:

- describe the project in a sentence or two;
- understand the sequence of work;
- keep a mental checklist of your specific responsibilities; and
- know who to network with outside the team.

THE FIVE PHASES OF FLIGHT

THE FLIGHT

You are going to Washington, D.C., next week. You made reservations, set up meetings, and otherwise prepare in the midst of other activities.

A few hours before the flight, you begin a new phase of this journey. Between being home and being airborne lie a number of hurdles: traffic to the airport; an unexpectedly full parking garage; the momentary panic when you think you've forgotten your tickets; lines at the reservations counter, lines at the security gate, lines at the boarding gate, where you discover the delay in your flight. An hour later than you expected, you strap yourself in and the plane heads out to the runway. In one breathtaking instant, the takeoff phase is over and you are in flight.

The flight itself is the bulk of the journey. Although it doesn't feel that way, it's where you do the real work of getting from here to there. Information during the flight comes from the crew in the cockpit, where they monitor sensors and adjust controls. The crew adapts to such variables as weather, traffic, and malfunctions by making changes in flight, with the ultimate objective of a safe landing, ideally at the scheduled destination.

"In preparation for landing, please make sure that your seat belts are securely fastened and that your seat backs are in their full upright position with your tray tables stowed." The flight attendant signals the start of the next phase, the process of landing. Landing and takeoff are the most stressful and dangerous events within the flight process. Hitting the ground almost always jars. The actual arrival at the airport presents another set of obstacles—getting to a clear gate, collecting your baggage, and finding a taxi.

Finally, with the flight complete, you arrive at your destination with a new status quo established. Thinking ahead (and remembering the morning's delay), you decide to confirm your flight home and inquire about times for that trip to the islands you have been thinking about. You are at the beginning of the next journey even as you arrive.

THE FIVE PHASES

The five phases of flight are a metaphor for the five phases of teamnets.

- Prepare   • Startup
- Takeoff   • Launch
- Flight   • Perform
- Land   • Test
- Arrive   • Deliver

Two periods of predictable turbulence—takeoff/launch and land/test—fall between the beginning (prepare/startup), middle (flight/perform), and end (arrive/deliver). Teamnets also experience these periods of turbulence in their development, which you can anticipate and use to advantage.

Launch follows a sometimes lengthy startup period, and usually involves a relatively short but intense activity set that produces a plan and defines leadership. Perform is the growth period of activity, where tasks are undertaken and results accumulate. But growth is always limited, and deadlines always loom. Work must be tested, brought in for a sometimes dangerous "landing," delivered to customers, and rolled out to users. A new status quo comes with the achievement of a destination that the next cycle of change will challenge.

Little journeys are contained within bigger journeys that are part of greater journeys, or "vision quests." Startup to delivery may happen over a matter of days, or the process may take years to unfold.

- *Startup:* Long or short, in the initial period people assess and gather information. Anomalies accumulate as people speak out and ideas are tested.
- *Launch:* At some point, things jell—or they don't. Many teamnets require a spark of creativity, a group "Aha" that cements a core belief. Here is where the group feels itself click and people begin to refer to themselves as "we."
- *Perform:* If only we could live here permanently. People engage their energy and take huge strides in accomplishing real work as the overall effort achieves its objectives. There are problems and challenges, to be sure, but problem solving is the modus operandi.
- *Test:* Risks converge here. Success may blind us, and we may exceed the carrying capacity of our environment. The innovation undergoes strenuous testing before acceptance. Forces of resistance mount their final assault.
- *Deliver:* The process passes a final milestone. Here the process may end, stabilize at a new status quo, or go into another cycle.

THINKING THROUGH THE PHASES

The art of developing networks comes from combining the five *principles* with the five *phases*. An approach to the startup phase is described in the section "Startup: Assessing the Situation." "Launch: Planning the Work" outlines using the principles in the launch phase.[3]

The Five Teamnet Principles operate as a failure detector in the perform phase. Anticipate where the group is likely to get into trouble, where its weaknesses are going to show. We describe these elements as "warnings" in our introduction to the principles in chapter 4.

Network organizations grow in a turbulent sea of change. Maintaining a goal-oriented direction requires constant adjustments of the major elements of the network. Balance the cooperative principles—unifying purpose and voluntary links—with the competitive principles—independent members and multiple leaders. Co-opetition is a dynamic flow, not a steady state.

TEAMNET ACTION MATRIX

PURPOSE:	GOALS $\longrightarrow$		TASKS $\longrightarrow$		RESULTS
Phases *5 Principles*	STARTUP	LAUNCH	PERFORM	TEST	DELIVER
PURPOSE	Common View?	Clarify Purpose	Glueless–Groupthink	Test Results	Deliver Results
MEMBERS	Colleagues?	Identify Members	Dependent–Stubborn	Member Reviews	Member Results
LINKS	Connections?	Establish Links	Isolated–Overload	Feedback Relations	Ongoing Connect
LEADERS	Voices?	Multiply Leaders	Leaderless–Followerless	Succession	New Leaders
LEVELS	Inclusion?	Integrate Levels	No Uplinks–No Downlinks	Travel Levels	New Level
Analogy	PREPARE	TAKEOFF	FLIGHT	LAND	ARRIVE

CHECKING IT OUT

People know well the turbulence of the launch phase. Most experienced consultants and managers know the difficulties involved in catalyzing a group to initiate any change process. Less well known is the second anticipatable point of stress, the test phase, which is the transition from the task-oriented perform phase to the results-oriented delivery phase.

The test phase is that downstream place where the upstream planning effort pays off. You can apply criteria for success based on goals established here. If you involve downstream players in the initial planning, you can turn this phase into a cakewalk instead of the nightmare it sometimes becomes when customers (internal or external) see unsatisfactory results coming at them. Typically, the network, in its broadest form, gets involved across the levels in reviews and other examinations of the result. Feedback becomes a conscious activity, not just a loop of communication.

Like the launch phase, this transition tests leaders. Often there is a need for succession, a passing of the baton:

- Along the value chain from supplier to customer;
- From one generation to another; or
- From the managers of a development effort to the owners of a new status quo.

A teamnet is not truly tested until it grows beyond the leaders who initiated it and originally propelled its development.

DELIVERING THE GOODS

Networks are as much processes of organization as they are structures. Because purpose is their source of legitimacy, an essential part of the life cycle of teamnets is the delivery phase. Without results, there is no reason to continue to maintain relationships.

Since a network comprises its members and their relationships, the members themselves must each get whatever they need from the situation. This is true whether it means being able to anticipate future benefit or feeling good about a contribution to the whole. Two sets of measures gauge results in a network: those of the teamnet as a whole and those of each member. How members measure results is an essential part of building (or tearing down) trust and the ability of this network or others to function in the future. Will the connections be ongoing? Will a new steady state retain vitality and a capacity for change?

Networks may be transitory, like a cross-functional team, or effectively immortal, like the medical profession. Delivery for some teamnets means, well, "death" for the organization. The passing of a set of relationships often requires some grieving or celebrating. One cross-company teamnet charged with developing a convergence plan for five competing products held an end-of-project dinner at its successful completion in barely six weeks. Simply acknowledging that a project has died can aid people in the grieving process.[4]

The completion of a life cycle is often the beginning of a new one. New leaders represent new seeds of teamnet growth and new phases of activity.

CHAPTER 6

THE HINGE OF HISTORY: ASSESSING YOUR TEAMNET POTENTIAL

REINVENTING GOVERNMENT WITH NETRESULTS

In Washington, D.C., the National Museum of American History houses a very interesting exhibit of bureaucratic change. It heralds the start of the Information Revolution. A woman standing in a 19th-century office literally *cuts red tape* while a man in Victorian business suit watches. She is liberating brown accordion folders full of papers, held together by red tape, the prevailing mode of storage since the end of the 17th century. On this day, the organization of information took its next great leap—into the newly invented wooden filing cabinet.

"Bureaucracy," a word first used by Thomas Carlyle, who called it the "continental nuisance" in 1848, institutionalized the storage of information, embodied in the written word. In fact, the now extinct root word *burel* meant a writing desk. This treatment of written material, in which ideas are physically encased, typically with only private access, is quite different from its treatment in networks, where "information wants to be free."[1]

Appropriately, in August, 1993, the seeds of the networking of one of the world's largest bureaucracies, the U.S. government, may have been planted just across the street from the museum on Constitution Avenue.

On a steamy end-of-August dog day, most people in the capital had

127

left for vacation. Yet the vestibule of the Mellon Auditorium, with its three-story-tall marble columns and oak floors so old that they can no longer be sanded, was crowded and noisy with 200 people.

They were registering for a conference. Its purpose? To launch a network of federal employees committed to "reinventing government." We were there as designers and facilitators of the three-day getting-started process.

Reinvent government? Is this possible? It sounds like the proverbial oxymoron. Even if you could, skeptics say, would you want to? U.S. Vice President Al Gore decided to try. "Latest Plan to Make Government Work Just Might Work," said *The Wall Street Journal* in its page 1, right-hand-column lead story on the day Gore handed his report[2] to the president in full South Lawn ceremony dress. Gore's effort got a similar response from all the major media, even though it reportedly was somewhere between the 11th and 500th study of how to tame the federal bureaucracy beast.

It is big. The U.S. government employs 2.2 million people, *not* including the military. It spent $2.1 trillion in its 1994 fiscal year. It does not move quickly or gracefully. Meanwhile, it employs some of the most intelligent, creative people in the country, many dedicated to superb government service.

The United States is not the only country looking at reinvention. Australia, Canada, Denmark, Great Britain, France, Sweden, and New Zealand, as well as a few less likely candidates—Italy, Mexico, India, Chile, Palestine, South Africa, and Germany—are but a few countries that are reinventing. Virtually every state in the Union has some type of reinvention effort underway, as do hundreds of cities and towns, including such differing places as New York City and Youngstown, Ohio.[3] Even tiny Sanford, Maine, where Gordon Paul, the chief of police, has become an expert in quality and networking.

All this governmental introspection is easy to understand. Like most other centuries'-old organizations, the U.S. government can no longer cope with its problems in the same way it has in the past. Andy Campbell, an organization development specialist at none other than the Central Intelligence Agency (which also went under the reinvention microscope), adapts a quote from Einstein: "We can't solve the problems of the 21st century with 19th-century organizations."[4]

The 21st century is about speed and information, knowledge and competence, complexity and wisdom. The 19th century was about slow, steady progress, factories and railroads, clockworks and mechanisms. Industrial Age organizations ill serve the turmoil of the Age of the Network.

A REVIEW OF NATIONAL PERFORMANCE

Gore launched the effort to reinvent the U.S. government in March, 1993, by enlisting the help of 200 federal bureaucrats. Insiders, not consultants and outside experts, staffed the National Performance Review (NPR). This was a highly significant difference from previous government reform studies.

NPR had an exceptionally cross-boundary design. The 200 people formed 33 cross-functional teams, one for each major agency, numbering 22, and 11 cross-cutting "systems" teams looking at issues that spanned departmental boundaries.

The rule for the agency teams was that people could not work on their own department. Marion Metcalf, for example, a policy analyst in the Enforcement Office at the Department of Justice's Immigration and Naturalization Service, was a member of the Department of Labor Team. For the systems teams, "NPR recruited recognized reformers (by networking to find out who they were!)," Metcalf explains. Thus, Lynn Sandra Kahn, an organization development specialist at the Federal Aviation Authority, served on the Organizational Structures Team, and Vincette Goerl, a financial manager from the General Services Administration, worked on the Financial Management Team. A few people served as "special assistants," including Capt. Dennis Egan of the Commandant's Strategic Planning Force at the U.S. Coast Guard, whose work included the design for electronic distribution of the final report. Larry Koskinen, a career Peace Corps manager, worked on the NPR's U.S. Agency for International Development team, then continued with NPR as project manager for Gore's Internet-based electronic town hall.

This cross-boundary approach to reforming the government was a brand new idea. No one had ever tried it before, and no one was sure it would work. To complement this effort (and perhaps to hedge bets), each agency also set up its own internal reinvention team. For example, Metcalf's effort on the Department of Labor Team had its counterpart in-house. In some cases, the cross-functional teams interacted extensively with the departmental teams; in others, they barely spoke.

The beauty of this design was that it depended on the real experts— the people who, on a daily basis, grind out the federal government. No one knows better than they the pain of securing 23 signatures for a simple travel voucher or the labor-intensive process that can take up to three years to finalize a PC purchase. Several generations of PCs develop, grow, and die in that time.

Nor did NPR play ostrich and ignore the accumulated wisdom of the private sector. They invited numerous management consultants to address the staff at brown bag lunches and give keynote speeches. Tom Peters kicked off the Labor Department's reinvention effort with a packed house of 1,500 at the Mellon Auditorium. Joseph Juran, Peter Senge, Daryl Connor, and Shoshanna Zuboff, to name just a few, along with executives from many corporations coping with complex change, got their 15 minutes, many in front of Gore himself.

We got involved because Marion Metcalf had a sore throat. Our last book, *The TeamNet Factor*, was still in galley stage when Seattle-based Robert Gilman, publisher of *In Context* magazine, read it on a flight to Washington. When he arrived, he called Al Gilman (his brother and Marion's husband), who was at choir practice, which Marion had skipped due to her sore throat. So Marion and Robert started talking, and she explained her new assignment working for the vice president. The toughest problem, she said, was how to get agencies, as well as internal departments, to work together across boundaries. Robert told her about our book, and soon we too were volunteering some help to NPR.

LAUNCHING NETRESULTS

As the summer wore on and the report's deadline, September 7, loomed, people began to wonder what would happen when they returned to their home agencies. Their experience had turned them into evangelists. They looked at ways to improve the government and saw feasible solutions. How could they go back to, in many cases, their dreary, paper-pushing, meeting-infested, low-results jobs? Couldn't they stay connected in some way, continuing to exchange ideas while actively working to implement the recommendations?

By early August, Carolyn Lukensmeyer, NPR's deputy director, working with Andy Campbell and a handful of others, asked for our help in launching a *people network* to link the returning army of reinventing-government believers. Of the more than 600 people invited, some 200 showed up, and in the last week of August, 1993, NetResults[5] was launched in the Mellon Auditorium, where the president presents the Malcolm Baldrige National Quality Awards each year. By the end of the third day of the conference, the group had named itself, crafted a set of goals, expressed its preferences for how to communicate, developed a plan, and agreed upon a mission statement:

> *"To serve as a communication vehicle and catalyst to facilitate broad participation, stimulate leadership, and support the goals, strategies, activities, and achievements of continuous government improvement."*

Generic, perhaps, this statement was also sufficiently open-ended so that it can harbor many initiatives and tap the creativity of countless bureaucrats bursting with the energy to improve the government.

Operating only informally, and with such encouraging word-of-mouth approval as Gore's message on September 16, 1993, to go "full steam ahead"[6] with NetResults, the network soon linked 500 people in 50 agencies. It operates through face-to-face meetings, informal exchange of memos, and electronically. On the Internet[7] fly scads of conversations, manifold e-mail address lists, opinions, articles, drop-in chats, and online computer conferences.[8]

NetResults has also spawned numerous subnetworks addressing focused areas of critical concern to reinvention, including BudgetNet, concerned with the budgeting process; FinanceNet, examining financial management innovations; PeopleNet, looking at human resources reform; MeasureNet, identifying and inventing new types of performance measures; GrantsNet, linking the grants management organizations; IGnet, joining the Inspectors General across agency lines; and Social Services Web, aimed at delivery and integration among the social service agencies.

NetResults is itself only part of the alliance of governmental bodies involved in implementing reinvention, which includes the President's Management Council (largely comprising the COOs of the major agencies), the Federal Quality Institute, the management side of the Office of Management and Budget, and congressional reinvention allies on legislation, as well as a residual NPR staff. The efforts in the U.S. federal government are part of a larger reinvention movement involving localities, states, and other nations.

With NetResults as the point of reference, we can look both inward to its constituent parts and outward to the systems and environments that include it.

Will it all add up to anything? The "net result" remains to be seen, but already something new has happened, something that has never happened before at this scale with this sophisticated technology at the federal level.

NETRESULTS IN CONTEXT

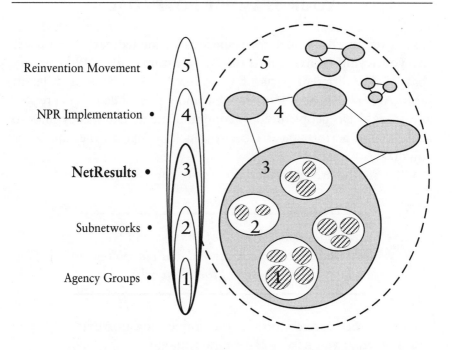

People are talking to one another, building trust, reaching across their stovepipes and silos, exchanging ideas and shortcuts, working faster, and thinking smarter.

If nothing else, NetResults has unleashed great creativity among people who want to improve government.

YOUR TEAMNET POTENTIAL

Is your organization, in some respects, like the federal government? Are you trying to move into the 21st century with a 19th-century chassis? Are different parts of your enterprise moving at different rates? Are some groups more flexible and agile, while others are stiff and stodgy? Do people need to communicate across agency lines to achieve high performance? Does so much change all the time leave you dizzy?

What are the drivers behind the Age of the Network?

Size and scope, the pace of change, and the coevolution of organizational and technological systems drive the Age of the Network.

Each of these drivers provides a simple indicator that helps you assess whether you need a 21st-century design.

- *Size and scope:* Any organization that is big and complex or that naturally works across boundaries needs networks.
- *Pace of change:* The faster the pace, the more flexible the organization needs to be. Is your pace of change accelerating?
- *Systems:* Organizations need both social and technology networks if they are spread out geographically, operate in different time zones, or include diverse cultures.

SIZE AND SCOPE: THE HIERARCHY RULER

Government is the archetype of the Industrial Age bureaucracy. This is natural, for governments are the granters of charters both public and private. Every incorporated organization registers with "the state."

Bureaucracies gain their legitimacy from constitutions, the source of law and all derivative legal systems.

So it should come as no surprise that government is the organizational sector most ruled by policies, regulations, and procedures. Specialization and departmental isolation are rampant. Robert Maslyn, director of special grants initiatives for the Department of Health and Human Services, calls it the "resident solo expert" problem: people who sit only a few feet apart often have no knowledge of what the other is doing.[9] Vertical functional stovepipes, so bemoaned in business, clog decision making and information flow.

Government, like every other sector, is spinning into the Information Age at an astonishingly accelerating rate, generating networked organizations in the process. Fueled by networked information systems, internal cross-agency networks like NetResults continue to multiply. Meanwhile, networks mushroom among governments in old areas such as trade and in new ones such as the environment.

Governments, particularly national ones, make exquisite network members. Nations—ideally independent, self-reliant, and integrated—enjoy sovereignty. At every level within nations—federal to state, state to municipality, municipality to school district—jurisdictions have sovereignty, with constraints set by the level above.

Sovereigns usually form a network when they agree to cooperate. In theory, no one's on top; everyone bears some responsibility. Boston and its surrounding localities have a fire-fighting mutual aid pact. Outside Portland, Maine, five school districts have joined in the Casco Bay Educational Alliance to enhance learning opportunities across the municipalities. The states in the Southeast are working together to increase exports; in the Southwest on border issues; in the Northwest on natural resource issues; in the Northeast on high energy costs. OPEC, NATO, SEATO, and NAFTA all are alliances among sovereigns formed to address common problems.

Shared purpose and mutual respect among independent partners are the basis for genuine, noncoercive government alliances. Governments are *very* sensitive to matters of sovereignty.

At the global level, the United Nations (UN), a bewildering bureaucracy, is logically and at its heart an inherently networked organization. As an association of sovereigns with both shared and competing interests, the UN embodies the essence of global co-opetition—competition and co-operation.

> *The drama of transition to the Age of the Network is stark here: the UN can further bloat and strangle as bureaucracy hopelessly multiples in the vain hope of "managing" complexity. Or it can reorganize, moving to become the natural network that it is, supported by global technologies.*

As the UN demonstrates, scope and size are not the same. Governmentally, the UN is a modestly sized bureaucracy, although given its affiliations with other global agencies, such as the World Bank, and with myriad nongovernmental organizations (NGOs), it has quite a reach beyond its official employee base of 30,000. Although a small player, the UN's scope is automatically global and transnational. Not itself the global whole, the UN nonetheless endeavors to represent it. It enables and supports a rich set of internation relationships that together make up a major portion of the global fabric.

Historically, trade has been the leading edge for the spread of innovations, causing business to generate a vast part of the global web of relationships. Large and small companies alike export or compete against exports, and most very large companies are multinational or are becoming so. Special interests cross all jurisdictions, reaching customers who are global. Even so, business does not have a formal seat on the Security Council. Everywhere, communication is instant, CNN is ever present, and people go global all the time.

Has your scope expanded? Do you have a distributed organization in any major part of your system—inputs, value-adding processes, or outputs? As the number of relationships increases, does the need for communication rise? Are your suppliers all local? Are your employees all in the same building? Are your customers dispersed? Your competitors?

GETTING A GRIP

To get a grip on size and scope, use what might appear to be the most unlikely systems principle: hierarchy. Here the term does not represent a social pyramid but rather the concept of sets within sets within sets (see chapter 3, "Turning Hierarchy on Its Side").

Every organization is made up of parts and is itself part of a larger whole. Wholes and parts[10] are gifts from the universe. They make it possible to simplify the complex.

To use this powerful principle, apply the "Hierarchy Ruler":

The key is to choose a point of reference.

THE HIERARCHY RULER

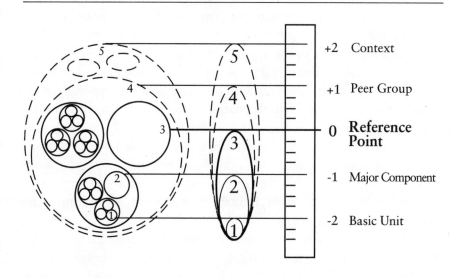

+2	Context
+1	Peer Group
0	**Reference Point**
-1	Major Component
-2	Basic Unit

The Hierarchy Ruler is one of the most useful mental tools you can ever employ. Set a reference point and then look both ways—internally and externally. Each boundary offers an opportunity for a two-way perspective, like that of Janus, the ancient Roman deity who could look both inside and outside at once from his palace entrance.

The corporate boundary is a good typical point of reference where you can take the CEO's view. The whole organization is your responsibility. From that boundary, you can see both the internal complexities—budgets, politics, love affairs—and the external ones—competitors, markets, global upheaval. With the reference point as an anchor:

- *Externally*, ask what significant relationships the anchor organization maintains. Look at other enterprises like yours, your peers, customers, and suppliers; further out, see the anchor organization in the context of whole industries and markets.
- *Internally*, ask what the anchor organization comprises. Look for the major components, the departments or divisions that tell the broad story of what the corporation does. Each internal division itself is made up of groups within groups within groups.

A ruler is a portable, general-purpose tool that can measure many things. Its anchor—its point of reference—is completely movable. Indeed, to tap a ruler's power, you *must* move the reference point.

On the Hierarchy Ruler, the anchor is in the middle instead of at one end. Place it at different boundaries to assess situations from other points of view. This is a critical cross-boundary networking skill that many people already use well intuitively.

Now move the reference point from the corporate boundary down to your department and drop it again to your team, and perhaps yet again to subgroups within the team. Or go up from the enterprise to alliances, coalitions, markets, industries and regions—ever wider circles of associations.

With Eastman Chemical Company as the reference point, for example, move up one level to see customer alliances and supplier-partner ties. Move up again and see the chemical industry as a whole, of which

Eastman is a part. Return to the company level anchor point, then move down one step to see its six major components (see Eastman Chemical Company's Organization Chart, chapter 3) and 42 business units. Go down another level to see the hundreds of vertical and horizontal teams. To see the level of individual people, move down again to the employees who make up the teams, units, components, and ultimately, the company as a whole.

Another example using the Hierarchy Ruler can be seen in the "NetResults in Context" diagram, moving from small groups up to the reinvention movement as a whole.

> *The teamnet itself embodies this valuable mental tool of levels within levels, a network whole composed of teams that are themselves complex.*

MOVING TO THE NEXT MACH

Vibrating at the tip of creative evolution, our world is the culmination of everything that has happened for billions of years. We carry not just traces of our past, but also its flesh and blood as evolution combines old features with the new ones that follow.

We are both past and future, existing in a creative human culture in which daily change hurls boulders of uncertainty in our paths. Change is often uncomfortable, it sometimes hurts, and it can even be fatal. Never before has the world had to cope with the pace of change that affects six billion of us every day. Collectively, we are struggling to learn the new survival skills of life in the Age of the Network.

Our past is very deep. Along with our specifically human heritage is our biological heritage, billions of years old. This biological awareness remains the staple of daily life, engaging our personal attention. Think of your interest in your health, your personal biology. Consider

THE BIG TIMELINE

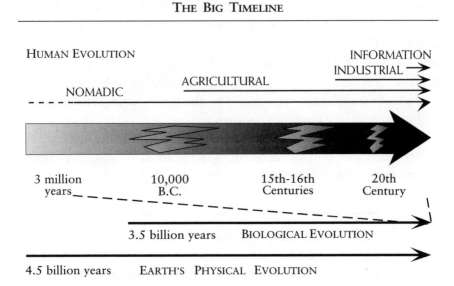

the enormous public concern with the health system, its economic impact on the cost of government, taxes, and budgets. Our social biology, represented most centrally by each person's own family, is also under enormous stress. Meanwhile, our biological home struggles with myriad environmental challenges.

Beyond our basic biology are the accumulating layers of our organizational life.

SCALE IN THE LONG VIEW

The Age of the Network is well underway as the 21st century dawns. Connections accelerate explosively worldwide. With *digital convergence*—the integration of computers, telephone, cable, information providers, and myriad other players—soon upon us, we're about to take another leap further into the Information Age.

Looking back, we need very different scales to measure the pace of change: eons, millennia, centuries, and decades.

- *Millions of years mark the Nomadic Age* of human history. A single person's life was very short—30 was old. Epochal changes were too far apart for any single person to notice them. Nevertheless, slowly over eons, people invented symbols, tools, and finally speech.

- *Millennia measure the Agricultural Age.* Agriculture became dominant 100 centuries before the birth of Christ, and its reign lasted until the end of the Middle Ages—the 15th to 16th centuries. The wheel and writing swept the known world, but rather slowly.
- *Centuries mark the Industrial Age,* from the Enlightenment to the mid-20th century. Rational science, machines, and printing powered this industrial engine. The pace of change for an individual's life speeded up, albeit at a measured, predictable, progressive rate. Still, a wheel with an engine is a much faster vehicle than a pushcart.
- *Now epochal change comes in decades.* Even before industrialism reached its peak in the mid-20th century, the conceptual shift from Newtonian to quantum physics sowed the seeds of the Fourth Age.[11] Three events in the last six months of 1945 herald its arrival. In half a year, nuclear power exploded on the world stage in Hiroshima and Nagasaki; scientists switched on ENIAC, the first electronic computer, in Philadelphia; and the United Nations Charter was signed in San Francisco. Since then, we have measured significant human change in decades and years.

In the 1970s, information workers surpassed manufacturing workers, just as factory hands once surpassed farm hands. Generations alive today straddle two eras, riding the Third Wave. Together, we inhabit both the old Industrial Age and the new Information Age. It is a difficult but exciting time to be alive. And it is a great responsibility which humanity doesn't get to do again.

At the first light of the 21st century, the baby boom, which started at the end of the Second World War, is in power, the first generation of the Information Age. These are the people of the 1960s generation who inaugurated the struggle between the two epochs, unleashing seismic shifts in values.

The complex global scale of modern business outstrips the capacity of the accumulated organizational wisdom of earlier ages. The overall

THE HINGE OF HISTORY

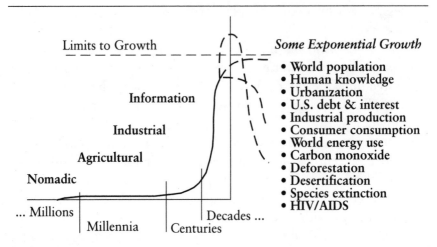

Limits to Growth
Some Exponential Growth

Information

Industrial

Agricultural

Nomadic

- World population
- Human knowledge
- Urbanization
- U.S. debt & interest
- Industrial production
- Consumer consumption
- World energy use
- Carbon monoxide
- Deforestation
- Desertification
- Species extinction
- HIV/AIDS

... Millions
Millennia
Decades ...
Centuries

pace of change drives the next form of organization in the Big Picture. New technology eventually brings the ability to manage in an increasingly larger context as more success brings more growth. Over the long span, the earth's population has grown at the same logarithmic rate as the pace of change.

Biophysicist John Platt, one of the early chroniclers of the pace of change, called our epoch the "hinge of history."[12] Everything shoots up the hockey stick curve of exponential growth in our time[13]—from population and ecological load to the spread of HIV/AIDS and the growth of knowledge. Such acceleration cannot be sustained indefinitely; there are always limits to growth.[14] Three general scenarios accompany the "S curve": overshoot and crash; undershoot and collapse; and restabilization at a higher level of civilization, definitely the best and smartest option.

PACE IMPACTS PATTERN

Eons, millennia, centuries, decades. The pace of change increases with each new age of human civilization as time shrinks.

Today businesses exist in multiple environments at once, each moving at a separate rate. Organizational environments have evolved from the simple and stable to the complex and unpredictable.[15]

Research since the late 1940s has shown that the pace of change in a business's environment greatly affects its organization. Typically, these studies place organizations along a yardstick that has "mechanistic" types at one end and "organic"[16] types at the other.

In general, slower change correlates with a more mechanistic organization, while faster change leads to a more organic one.

Speed impacts organizational type:

- Authority runs *mechanistic* organizations, with a strict chain commanding people who perform highly specialized jobs. Superiors pass instructions, decisions, and orders down to subordinates.
- *Organic* organizations, while they have authority structures, do not depend on them. Instead, people enjoy rich communication links that enable them to tolerate less clearly defined jobs. With consultation and broad access to information, self-control rather than top-down command is the *modus operandi*.

While hierarchy and bureaucracy are alive and well *and* needed, they are everywhere in consolidation. Relative to the "good old days," everyone feels the rush of change, which is rising so fast that in the minds of many, it appears out of control. Most companies, most groups, and organizations of every kind—from family to nation—are moving in relatively faster waters in this dizzy, speedy age. Each day more people meet even more people, finding themselves operating in more networks as we move deeper into the Information Age.

WHAT IS YOUR PACE OF CHANGE?

How do you apply these ideas to your organization? Do you have a mechanistic organization attempting unsuccessfully to operate in a turbulent environment? Is networking called for?

Not all work calls for networks. Are you trying to use a virtual networked team where a face-to-face fire-fighting unit would be more appropriate? Are essential infrastructure functions in jeopardy because the rush to flatten has decimated middle management? Have champions of companywide standards been silenced in the push for greater unit autonomy?

A teamnet solution does not have to start with a search-and-destroy mission. It looks for new power and synergies in connections, in distributing information and responsibility, in applying new network approaches to old management problems.

Compare the pace of change with the flexibility of structure to match work with the right organization.

Gauge the Environmental Speed

First, estimate the speed. There are many ways to appraise the pace of change; the following rule-of-thumb chart is just a start. Look at innovation, customer demand, competitors, and government policies.[17] Add variables, such as commodity prices or health care costs, to make the chart relevant to your specific situation.

Where does your organization appear on the range from stable to turbulent? Parts of larger organizations also move at different speeds. Imagine color-coding your organizational chart by the impact of the rate of change on each unit. Think also about your outside networks—with suppliers, customers, competitors, regulators, and reporters—and the velocity of change you experience there.

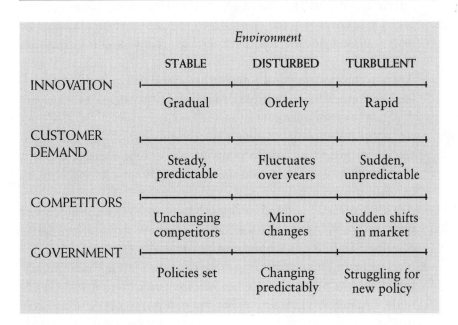

ENVIRONMENTAL PACE OF CHANGE ASSESSMENT

	Environment		
	STABLE	DISTURBED	TURBULENT
INNOVATION	Gradual	Orderly	Rapid
CUSTOMER DEMAND	Steady, predictable	Fluctuates over years	Sudden, unpredictable
COMPETITORS	Unchanging competitors	Minor changes	Sudden shifts in market
GOVERNMENT	Policies set	Changing predictably	Struggling for new policy

Evaluate the Type

Is your organization more mechanistic or more organic? Look at the organization in terms of the characteristics listed in the "Organizational Assessment" chart.

ORGANIZATIONAL ASSESSMENT

HIERARCHY-BUREAUCRACY *Mechanistic*		TEAM-NETWORK *Organic*
Extrinsic purpose		Intrinsic purpose
Imposed control		Self-control
Specialized		Generalized
Dependence		Independence
Formal channels		Voluntary relations
Commands		Consultation
Appointed leaders		Natural leaders
Formal jobs		Loosely defined jobs
Vertical interaction		Lateral interaction
Rigid levels		Flexible levels

- Does purpose always come from higher authorities or is there an internal source of purpose, a spark of independent, self-generated life? Does control come down from the top in vertical chains or does it arise from the self-control of associates seeking common results?
- Are the components and jobs in the organization highly special-ized or do they have multiple capabilities? Are the parts relatively dependent or independent?
- Are there only formal channels of communication, up and down the social hierarchy, or do people form voluntary relationships every which way? Is communication through channels or by consultation?
- Are all leaders appointed or does the group have natural leaders with authority? Are jobs formally or loosely defined (the latter offering flexibility and opportunity for leadership)?
- Is all interaction vertical or is there extensive lateral communica-tion along the plane of processes where work exists? Are the levels of the organization impermeable and maintained as rigid controls or are they continuously and flexibly re-forming to meet the needs of change and growing complexity?

No company is either unbendingly rigid or always flexible. Most organizations mix mechanistic and organic features. Imagine map-ping the parts color-coded to an organizational assessment.

Combine Time and Type

Compare your organizational assessment with your environmental pace of change; consider your mechanistic–organic maps against the stable–turbulent continuum. Together they provide a baseline for evaluating your large-scale teamnet opportunities and requirements.

A very stable environment with gradual innovation, predictable customer demand, the same competitors, and unchanging govern-ment policy would not be the first place to try a teamnet. And hold tight if you decide to plunge in at the other extreme. Don't be sur-prised to find some slow-moving organizations in fast-moving environments. Likewise, don't assume that just because some parts of the picture clearly need to be more networked, this solution is best everywhere.

TEAMNETS: THE ORGANIC SUCCESSOR TO HIERARCHY-BUREAUCRACY

As you sort out the appropriate mixes of organizational type to apply to your situation, you can compress this set of guidelines into a 2 × 2 matrix of simple–complex environments and mechanistic–organic organizations. Remember, however, that over the ages, organizational forms have accumulated. Older forms show up in some basic way in later forms.

ORGANIZATIONAL PAIRS

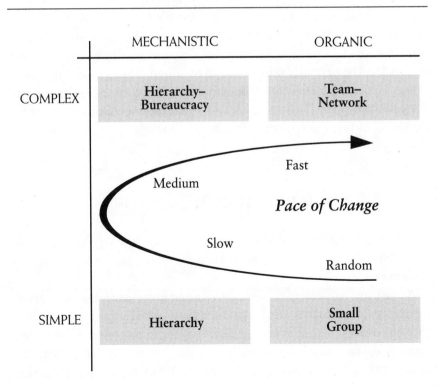

Simple environments. Small groups and hierarchies operate most effectively in environments where complexity is relatively low. On a daily basis, small groups deal with the vicissitudes of living and working. Their organic, self-organizing capabilities respond to the often chaotic, random changes of in-your-face everyday life. Where the environment is more predictable and size slows the rate of change, people can use simple command-and-control structures to manage larger-scale, fairly simple work.

Complex environments. Bureaucracy complements hierarchy; the two have clear organizational affinities. With commands and ranks, boxes and specialties, bureaucracy and hierarchy approach complexity like a machine. Specialization contributed by bureaucracy allows hierarchies to manage much more change and greater complexity. But when complexity accumulates and explodes, hierarchy-bureaucracy is woefully inadequate.

Teams and networks combine in complex environments, just as hierarchies and bureaucracies combine forces. The teamnet incorporates the team, the high-performing organic small group, with the network—the organic, multilevel, distributed metagroup. They both reflect basic structures and processes bound by a shared purpose and deep relationships. Teamnets are old and new, coevolving to meet the demands of fast-paced, changing, highly complex environments.

SOCIAL-TECHNICAL NETWORKS

Some organizations lead the journey into the Age of the Network. Their businesses are natural networks; their core technology is highly networked.

At Arthur Andersen & Co., like other large professional service businesses, the partners and associates are spread out across clusters of local offices. These firms are also leaders in applying information technology to knowledge work. Likewise, "service webs" spread out in natural networks—such as Domino's Pizza and other franchises that combine local entrepreneurism with extensive, distributed information systems. Hyatt Hotels manages a far-flung network of hotels and owners with integrated brand, marketing, and management skills.

From a technology perspective, process manufacturing requires more organic management than discrete manufacturing. The horizontal, networked nature of Eastman Chemical Company's work figuratively appears in the maze of pipes and tanks—processes and flows—of their production facilities. Federal Express created a network to provide a delivery service. AT&T's natural network technology, turned loose in the marketplace to face the full pace of change, has made it a leader among the giants in developing new ways of working. "AT&T is the most incredibly flexible large organization I've ever dealt with," says GO Corporation's CEO, Bill Campbell. "You don't need to go to committees. Somebody makes a decision, and we move on to the next one."[18]

While some organizations network more naturally than others, virtually all are incorporating new electronic technologies.

TECHNOLOGY OF THE INFORMATION AGE

With the invention of electronic circuits, the ideas of George Boole, Charles Babbage, Ada Lovelace, and others became the seminal technology for the Age of the Network. Chips, circuits, and satellites—the ever-expanding array of electronic devices—restructure old markets and open up new ones. Information, computer technologies, and global markets require networks. Hierarchy alone is too rigid, and bureaucracy is too slow.

- New ideas turn into new technologies.
- New technologies open up new economies.
- New ideas, technologies, and economies provoke new organizations.

Information technology first emerged at the peak of the Industrial Age. Not surprisingly, it looked appropriately mechanistic, and the

first few generations of computers were enormous. Their user inter-
faces were hideously complex and they were awesomely expensive,
available to only the largest institutions. The central computer—with
its professional priesthood, who alone understood its arcane
mysteries—needed to be shared to be cost effective, so it sprouted
dependent appendages, numbingly similar dumb terminals. The
whole system collapsed when the mainframe went down behind air-
conditioned glass walls set on raised floors.

Next came the chip. It leaked from the lab in the 1970s to the marketplace before anyone really knew what was happening. Instantly, a
revolution from below erupted with hobbyist kits like the Altair, gathered speed with the Apple II, and, finally exploded with the IBM PC.

Personal computers liberated the information revolution from
mainframe domination. PCs are an agent of personal empowerment
at the technological heart of the age. You and your computer are
independent members with autonomous capabilities, archetype nodes
in social/technology networks.

PCs linked into networks almost immediately. Networks have developed from a fringe curiosity to the central architecture of computing in
no more than a decade. PCs, linked into local area networks (LANs)
and wide area networks (WANs), as well as directly to the global
Internet, reflect the robustness of the network design. If the broader
networks go down, the local clusters still function. If local nets go
down, PCs and other devices continue to function and perform work.

A 1985 publication by Digital Equipment Corporation, then the
world's leader in developing networking technology, provided this
definition, still representative of this techno-genre:

> "A network comprises two or more intelligent
> devices linked in order to exchange information
> and share resources."

Here we see three essential elements of the Five Teamnet
Principles—nodes, links, and purpose. The nodes are the independent

SOCIAL-TECHNICAL NETWORKS

ORGANIZATION		TECHNOLOGY
Business goals & strategies	PURPOSES	Applications & solutions
Independent individuals or groups	NODES	Independent intelligent devices
Communications & relationships	LINKS	Physical network of connections
Members who coordinate	LEADERS	Servers and managers
Levels of work & organization	LEVELS	Levels of hardware & software

intelligent devices, the members. They are linked physically to serve purposes, the "in order to" of exchanging information and sharing resources. Networks come to life for a purpose, the business needs that specific applications meet.

Technology networks also reflect the last two of the five teamnet principles. Some nodes in technology networks serve as leaders—"servers," as they literally are known—which contain shared information, such as databases, and perform routing functions, such as delivering e-mail. Ironically, mainframes now have a renewed role in computer life as "servers" rather than "masters." Technology networks also make use of experts and administrators whose jobs are to maintain and protect the infrastructure, develop its capabilities, and resolve conflicts.

Levels appear throughout computer technology—hardware, software, and wiring schemes alike. At the user interface, hierarchical menus offer people the means to interact with a "machine" made of chips constructed from ephemeral Boolean logic gates—sets within sets within sets.

MAKING YOUR ASSESSMENT

Should your organization be using networks? Size and scope, the environmental pace of change, and social-technical infrastructures all shape the answer to that question.

We wish we had a formula to combine these factors and come up with definitive answers. We have no formula, but we can suggest some general rules of thumb for making quick assessments. Approximations, however, can be dangerous if used without experience and local knowledge. With that in mind, we also offer an approach for making a more detailed assessment in each of the three areas.

- *Networks are called for when the size is very large or when the scope is large and the size is small.*

Very large organizations, like multinational corporations, governments in alliance, and grass-roots movements, form networks because traditional hierarchy-bureaucracy simply cannot cope with the sheer magnitude of change. The issue for most organizations, however, is one of size relative to scope, which is determined by the purpose. In short, *we need networks when we want to do more than we can do alone, achieving results across boundaries in circumstances we can influence but cannot control.*

Evaluate the strategic advantages by exploring the levels that the organization touches for a more detailed assessment of size and scope. The Hierarchy Ruler helps you lay out your specific topography of size and scope, giving you a natural language for describing the complexity of your business.

> • *The faster the pace of change in the*
> *environment, the more organ-izations need*
> *organ-ic forms—teamnets.*

Broadly speaking, faster change correlates with more organic orga-nization. However, teamnets are not always the answer to speed. Certain situations cry out for hierarchy. Place your environmental speed "gauge" alongside your type assessment. Now use the two gauges at different levels within your organization. By color-coding your results, you have a vivid display of your organization's speed and type at many different levels.

> • *Draw a picture showing who you work with*
> *or how you do your work. Are there many*
> *circles and connecting lines? If so, you have*
> *opportunities for a natural network.*

Many organizations are natural networks or have become so through redesign. Both business process reengineering and quality initiatives often reorganize work into more horizontal, cross-boundary designs. A physically distributed business invites and re-quires distributed management techniques, as does a networked core technology.

To make a more detailed assessment of the network potential at the juncture of your organization and technology, apply the Five Teamnet Principles to both. To determine the areas of maximum strategic advantage, match the startup and launch results outlined in chapter 5 with a technology network assessment using the five-principle model. Then develop a change strategy that allows the organization to gain maximum productive advantage from the technology. Or draft a new technology plan that supports a work process that maximizes organizational advantage.

In the next chapter, as we take a ride on the Internet, we explore further the conjunction of people and technology and the power it releases.

SECTION IV

EXPANDING LINKS

Links, the focus of the next two chapters, are the signature characteristic of networks. Connections always have been important to organizations, but comparatively speaking, until recently, people have had limited links. In the past, the physical connections among people were relatively scarce and costly. To maintain control and enhance efficiency, hierarchy and bureaucracy minimize connections.

Links are not *new* in networks, but their variety and intensity are new, as is their use as a dominant design principle. New media that instantly circumnavigate our small planet bring with them geographically distributed organizations, virtual teams—and overloaded people.

"Only Connect," chapter 7, explores further the link between technology and people—from physical connections to interactions to relationships. We begin with the Internet, a phenomenon of the Age of the Network, both technical and social. Then we profile a new leadership role forming in cyberspace to help turn connections into relationships, one personified by Lisa Kimball, a skilled "networker." This coordinator role, however, generally appears in social networks of all kinds, which the extraordinary Elizabeth Meyer Lorentz classically exemplifies.

In "Social Capital," chapter 8, we go deeper—to the realms of trust, reciprocity, and communities, where people connect tightly. More remarkable is the glint of gold hidden in a thicket of relationships. Starting with an example 800 years in the making, today reflected in such areas as Silicon Valley and within organizations such as Eastman Chemical Company, we show the astonishing economic value of links.

CHAPTER 7

"ONLY CONNECT": THE IMPERATIVE OF THE 21ST CENTURY

> *Only connect! That was the whole of her sermon. Only connect the prose and the passion, and both will be exalted, and human love will be seen at its height. Live in fragments no longer. Only connect, and the beast and the monk, robbed of the isolation that is life to either, will die.*
>
> Howards End *by E.M. Forster*[1]

Something entirely new is wrapped around our planet—a way for one person to communicate with many at a very low cost, regardless of where they are in time or space. Spontaneously and with little planning, a global conversation and an information freeway have erupted in less than a decade, making next-door neighbors of people in Pottstown, Pennsylvania, Bangalore, India, and Johannesburg, South Africa. No single organization owns the Internet, the earth's interconnected computer network of networks. No authoritative hierarchy governs it. And it is growing faster than ever predicted.

The Internet is an electronic technology that makes it possible for people to "only connect." The Age of the Network is all about the ability to develop relationships that cross space and time. Geography need no longer be a barrier to people's capacity to work together and form communities.

The technology network *supports* the people network. Those who regard the technology alone as the network miss the point. Networking means people connecting with people, which happens whether they're sitting around a conference table, pressing their ear to the phone, staring at a computer, or standing by the fax machine.

The really fascinating technology story occurs when people engage at their deepest levels, solving problems, describing experiences, and allowing their "creative juices to really flow."[2]

THE INTERNET WORM

On November 2, 1988, a graduate student at Cornell University released the first big virus[3] on to the Internet. Launched at 5:01:59 P.M., the "Internet Worm" invaded a certain type of operating system on computers attached to the Internet—from Lincoln Labs and the National Supercomputer Center to Boston University and the University of California at San Diego. It shut down many big research sites and universities within the first hour.

Instantly, a spontaneous, geographically distributed, volunteer army of specialists, which we call "VirusNet," erupted to work round the clock to stop the worm, which they did in barely a day—not, however, before headline news had alarmed the public that World War III might be upon us.

VirusNet Self-organizes

VirusNet provides a classic study in the impromptu development of a laser-focused, mach-speed, emergency rescue network that achieved its objective—just like that. It demonstrates all five teamnet principles:

- VirusNet's clear *purpose* was to kill the worm.
- Everyone involved—perhaps a dozen at the core, with scores and ultimately hundreds of other minor players—was an *independent member.* If any single person left, VirusNet still survived.
- They communicated like crazy. They were richly *linked,* with intense face-to-face encounters. Countless phone calls skidded down lines of preexisting trust. And the physical Internet played its part: on the 95 percent of it not affected by the worm, people sent messages, swapped files, called up programs, and accessed databases.
- There were no bosses. *Multiple leaders* brought their expertise to bear at critical moments. No single person solved the problem; everyone together did.
- By the time it was over, VirusNet had engaged all the levels: the hierarchy *and* the lower-archy. While the computer labs hacked out the solutions, the press was in the office of MIT's vice president of information services. Within a week, the previously anonymous computer labsters who cracked the code found themselves in a debriefing with officials from the National Institute of Standards and Technology, the Defense Communications Agency, the Defense Advanced Research Projects Agency, the Department of Energy, the Ballistics Research Laboratory, the Lawrence Livermore National Laboratory, the Central Intelligence Agency, the Federal Bureau of Investigation, and the National Computer Security Center.

While destructive viruses have been loose in the computer world for at least a decade, this was the first *networking* worm. It posed as an imposter to linked computer systems and, once inside, went on to "propagate copies of itself."[4] Strange as it may seem, it was a relatively harmless worm. It only attacked computers running a specific operating system called Unix, the Bell Labs invention that blew open the potential for open systems and large-scale electronic networking.

Although the worm did not harm data or reveal any passwords, it did cause quite a ruckus. First, it had no business invading other machines to begin with. Once it arrived, it generated garbage through-out the whole system. It had to be stopped.

Robert T. Morris, Jr., was the Cornell student who unleashed the worm and eventually received one year's probation, along with 400 hours of community service and a $10,000 fine for his crime. Was it an accident that he chose the eve of the annual face-to-face meeting of Unix experts in Berkeley, California, to release it? This rare conver-gence brought together many of the world's best Unix minds. In any case, the network as a whole learned how to stop the worm in the snap-of-a-finger time of 36 hours.

The worm was not so much discovered by one person; as it was detected by many people at the same time. They figured out that it was a worm by putting their heads together. Within an hour of its launch, someone saw something strange on an MIT computer but couldn't figure out what it was. The first message calling it a virus came from someone at NASA's Ames Research Center nine hours after its release, saying the worm had attacked machines at the University of Califor-nia at Berkeley, University of California at San Diego, Lawrence Livermore National Laboratory, Stanford, and Ames. An hour later, someone at Harvard suggested that the worm was an Internet prob-lem. Within the next hour, more heads went up at separate sites at MIT, Berkeley, Brown, and SRI International.

Immediately, different groups of people in different labs went to work, forsaking sleep, food, and showers. Each lab went after the part of the problem that it knew best how to solve.

- One discovered a bug in the worm program that could be used against it.
- Another noticed that the worm crawled in through a wide open door, a particularly vulnerable bit of computer code,[5] and pub-lished a way to close it by midnight of the day after the worm's launch.
- Others replicated the worm on a "trenched" (isolated) machine, set off from the Internet so that it could only worm across its own experiment.
- Morris himself reportedly tried to kill the worm. According to

one account, he regretted his act almost immediately and, within a few hours of the release, asked a friend to post his solution on a computer bulletin board. However, no one could access it because the computer systems that needed to see Morris's message were the very ones that were down.

The weary labsters communicated continuously and extensively among themselves about their progress—both on the phone and through other network gateways not shut down by the worm. Occasionally, they went out to meals. In all, only eight days passed until every affected computer was back up and running, with no more than 4,000 machines infected in total, about five percent of the 80,000 then connected to the Internet (in mid-1994, 2,200,000 machines were connected).

PRESS AND PERCEPTIONS

Released on Tuesday, the worm problem had been solved by the time MIT hosted the first national press conference on Friday. The reporters were disappointed.

They had hoped for a much bigger story, perhaps one in which all the world's computers had been wiped out in a single moment, "that we were . . . moments away from World War III, or that there were . . . large numbers of companies and banks hooked up to 'MIT's network,' who were going to be really upset when Monday morning rolled around," wrote Jon Rochlis and Mark Eichin in their firsthand account of cracking the worm code.[6] "My greatest fear was that of seeing a *National Inquirer* headline: 'Computer Virus Escapes to Humans, 96 Killed,' " one labster said.

The media also were disappointed with the virus's lack of visuals, having to settle for people "looking at workstations talking 'computer talk.' " Much of the news is invisible to the camera's eye in the Age of the Network.

In fingering Morris as the chief suspect on the morning of the press conference, *The New York Times* reported the great irony of this story: "The enemy is us," in Rochlis and Eichin's words. It wasn't a terrorist operating out of some distant, strange land, or a corporate blackmailer, or a disgruntled worker who perpetrated the crime. It was a graduate student in computer science at a respected American institution whose father, Robert T. Morris, Sr., was the chief scientist at the National Computer Security Center.

While the worm did very little real damage, it revealed the vulnerability of the Internet at the same time as it unveiled its strengths. Chief among these is the design of the Internet, founded on the principle of "decentralizing defenses"[7]: don't protect the network; protect the individual nodes on the network.

This tightly couples to the final networking lesson taught by the worm:

> *In a complex, unpredictable world, diversity is the great armor of the whole fabric.*

Since the virus attacked only one type of computer operating system, few sites were put out of business completely. By having many different types of computer systems, the labs were safer than if their systems were all the same.

Diversity is safer, as well as smarter.

GOVERNING THE INTERNET

The Internet is an extraordinary example of network "governance." "It's anarchy that works," writes Norris Parker Smith.[8]

No one, no single institution, controls the Internet, particularly remarkable given that the Defense Advanced Research Projects Agency (DARPA), now known just as ARPA, started this network of networks almost three decades ago. Most of the military research money that went to major universities and corporations came from

DARPA. The agency connected its client research sites into a network built to withstand nuclear strikes or any other kind of catastrophe.

DARPAnet's architecture, its underlying philosophy of survival, was simple: every computer would be a peer, every machine simultaneously a source and a destination. Nodes on the Internet would act as independent senders and receivers but would also serve as intermediaries, as part of the infrastructure itself. It was taken for granted that the network would be unreliable. No critical "centers" were created, so none could be disabled. Both conceptually and in practice, this made for a very, very decentralized system.

In the late 1980s, the National Science Foundation used the "Internet Protocol," a soon to become famous set of computer standards for transferring information, to connect its five supercomputer centers. This "backbone," as the high-capacity skeleton of a computer network is called, which merged with DARPAnet, allowed a large number of local educational institutions to chain together and connect to it. *Voila*! Elite access of the few suddenly gave way to the great electronic masses, bursting with activity in hundreds of computer labs. The genie was out of the bottle, and the Internet spread big time.

Constituent parts of the Internet—short for "inter network," meaning between networks—are themselves networks many levels deep. Each computer that connects directly to the Internet is called a "domain," which itself may be a net within a net within a net. The Internet address that you see on TV's *Dateline*, for example, is a net within a net: dateline@news.nbc.ge.com.[9]

- Its code begins with *Dateline*, a particular addressee's name.
- The @ sign tells you where the computer is situated, in this case at NBC News.
- News is a part of the larger NBC Network, as in .nbc, pronounced "dot NBC."
- NBC itself is part of the giant General Electric, .ge.
- The .com on the end means that it's a commercial site on the Internet. MIT and most other educational institutions use .edu as their "last name." Most countries use their international country

code as their "last name:" for example, .in for India, .fr for France, and (still) .su for Russia.

But even the Internet's naming system is under discussion, which brings us to how the Internet really is governed.

Most of the governance is at the member level, and these internal variations differ in the extreme. Some members of the Internet are structured and controlled quite hierarchically (i.e., the military), some are more bureaucratically compartmentalized (i.e., educational institutions), and some are like teamnets (i.e., Silicon Valley companies). They may be authoritarian or communitarian, tightly controlled or welcoming to all. Control is largely local.

The "highest authority" is the Internet Society (ISOC), a *voluntary* membership organization. ISOC, in turn, appoints the Internet Architecture Board. This prestigious body of volunteers has great responsibility, setting common network standards and ensuring that addresses are unique: There cannot be two dateline@news.nbc.ge.com addresses on the Internet. The Internet Engineering Task Force deals with technical problems and near-term issues. When needed, a "working group" convenes to address a problem and provide information or recommendations as appropriate; then, just as quickly, it disbands.

Internet governance is a dramatic real-world example of a very-large-scale, self-organized network.

The Internet emerges from the heart of the Age of the Network, where physical connections converge and relationships grow, where pipes (computer lingo for the wires that connect) and personalities come together.

To think that a vital global facility serving millions of people is completely self-organized! And, oh, the freedom it gives.

Being online is not abstract. It is concrete, practical, and can be very personal.

A FEW HOURS IN THE LIFE OF AN ONLINE JUNKIE

For the first time in human history, we can live out E.M. Forster's 1943 advice to "Only connect!" The 21st century is about multiple connections on a global scale.

At this level the world is entirely networked, but unevenly so. Villages in China that don't have refrigerators have cellular phone uplinks. It's easier to send e-mail from Pushchino, Russia, than it is to fax. Meanwhile, our neighbors in West Newton, Massachusetts, operate with no such technology—they don't have a modem or even call waiting, for that matter—yet they bring new meaning to globe trotting: they're in Belize one week, in Taipei and Borneo the next, and in the south of France a month after that.

Computers today are highly personal. They support both introverts and extroverts, inner worlds and outer worlds. We (J&J) represent two poles of what awaits us in the 21st century. One of us works at an extremely high level of personal productivity without often going online; the other works with a different mix of technologies but communicates with many people around the world. Technology mushrooms with ever higher capacity in increasingly smaller packages, while people join new transborder communities without ever leaving home.

In a report on one session of Jessica's electronic meanderings, you'll see many uses of the Internet, from pure business to the most personal—none of it possible even a decade ago.

"Do Not Even Think of Touching This Modem"

It is early in the morning, and three messages are waiting from Duke University's Prof. Frank Starmer in my e-mail account on The World, a Boston computer system that offers Internet access. Remember the cardiologist/computer scientist with the lab without walls, based in

Madras, India, for the 1993–94 school year whom we introduced in chapter 1?

Frank, who lives the pain-pleasure nightmare of life in the electronic universe, is in a bit of a state. One small problem hampers communication of a basic breakthrough in his scientific research: last week, the 200-megawatt nuclear power station in South India failed.

"All of Madras was without power for 4–5 hours on Tuesday and then again on Wednesday. On Thursday night, a voltage spike took out our UPS [uninterruptable power supply] system, a transformer that powered the PC and the modem," which destroyed his modem in the process. Without his modem, Frank cannot communicate with his colleagues in France, Russia, Spain, and the United States, who wait anxiously for him to transmit key data from his lab experiments. All agree that they have made a significant discovery. They've pinpointed the origin of "a particular cardiac rhythm disturbance called *torsade de pointes*."

So, Frank has had to improvise. He has crawled around in closets and resurrected an old, half-working, 1200-baud modem ("If you even look at it cross-eyed, it fails"), which he has balanced on top of his PC. It has but one tragic defect. While it can probably survive something close to a nuclear meltdown, it has trouble detecting signals from down the street. This is not a trivial problem. A modem that can't hear a local signal is like a car without an engine—all dressed up with nowhere to go.

Hence the importance of Frank's sign on top of his PC: "Do not even think of touching this modem."

Enterprising fellow that he is, Frank has come up with another workaround. He has a backup Internet address that he can reach if he goes to another lab and "telnets" to his other account. Gibberish? Not to the 20–30 million people already on the Internet and the projected possibility of several hundred million more by the year 2000. For the Internet uninitiated, here's how it works. "Telnet" means nothing more than dialing another telephone number on the network, only with letters rather than numbers.

After conveying my sympathetic reply to Frank's plight, I leave my e-mail account to log on to MetaNet, a 10-year-old computer conferencing system based in Arlington, Virginia. To get there, I simply type "telnet tmn.com," and instantly I am logged in.

"Dead Too Soon"

MetaNet, like The Well in San Francisco and, on a grander scale, America Online, CompuServe, and Prodigy, allows groups of people to read and respond to the same information. Computer conferencing goes on in every conceivable discipline, on every imaginable topic, and at every level of sophistication. The MetaNet is host to many conferences. Next, I check in on a compelling one.

Suddenly, with a few more keystrokes, I am reading words that come from the ground-floor home office of Doug Lea, a 51-year-old "writer and thinker," as his electronic profile reads, and former presidential speech writer. With its "heavy 1790 wood beams, stone walls, and a walk-in fireplace,"[10] Doug's office too combines the very old with the very new. His Prometheus ProModem connects him to the rest of the world.

Occasionally, he mutters something that he's read on the screen to his wife, Julie, an award-winning artist, who has just come in from the gardens outside, lovingly tended here for many years by both of them in Waterford, Virginia, one of only three declared National Historic Landmark communities in the United States.

But there is something terribly wrong with this picture. The reason we're here with Doug and Julie is that Zack, their radiantly gifted son, is "dead too soon," as their poet neighbor wrote for his funeral, killed just shy of his 23rd birthday by an under-age drunk driver.

Doug is grieving in public on the network, posting his thoughts in a MetaNet conference where others can contribute to them, and he has attracted a crowd, including Stephanie Tolan, a novelist from the Midwest, who likens his following to a pod of dolphins: when one is ill, the others swim close by. As he is healing, others are telling fragments of deep tragedies that interweave one with the other, which Doug calls "a mobius."

Days go by and Doug says nothing, then suddenly he adds a long stream of interconnected memories and family snapshots, spurred by a new event. Today's is an unexpected letter from Zack's mentor at his boarding school, from which he graduated laden with awards, medals, and scholarships, both athletic and academic. Doug posts the letter to the network, adding his report on other Zack-related events from the past few days, including the brief story of a cruel remark delivered by a neighbor, and the pod moves in. A flurry of notes from others, one from a man who speaks supportively, though only sparsely and apologetically, because he "can't find words." Doug's ability to find words for enduring grief magically circles this community.

CRUISING TO BIG QUESTIONS

An important feature of the 21st century is that context shifts at the speed of light. A few keystrokes more and I'm attending a completely different conference, where the subject is design. Here the conversation focuses on the work of Christopher Alexander, the Austrian-born architect, now at the University of California at Berkeley, who has developed what he calls a "pattern language" for building desks, houses, schools, offices, and whole communities.[11] Lyn Montague, a high school English teacher from Newton, Massachusetts, and an expert on Alexander's work, leads the discussion. Then, more keystrokes:

- Respond to a client's e-mail.
- Read the agenda for an upcoming meeting of NetResults coordinators (see chapter 6).
- Retrieve Vice President Al Gore's speech on the information superhighway from the U.S. Department of Agriculture's online public area (called a "gopher").
- Post an answer to a technical question on an electronic bulletin board.
- Send a message to the *Utne Reader*, a Minneapolis, Minnesota-based magazine, inquiring about its online "e-salons."[12]

- Take a breather on the Internet Relay Channels, where people from all around the world drop in at their leisure, exchanging witty remarks and supportive words. This channel, called "#30plus," was dreamed up in an outdoor restaurant on the quay next to the Sydney Opera House by Helen Webberly, a professor of medieval art history at the University of Melbourne, Australia, and Daniel Ben-Safer, head of computer studies at Sydney's Metropolitan Business College (founded in 1895). "Heloise" (Helen's computer nickname) was "fed up with the macho, testosterone-ridden tone" of most of the chat channels and wanted to start one for "older" people. Thus its name—#30plus. Daniel ("Dabas," as he's known online), the other cofounder of #30plus, tells a different story: he says they were tired of hearing people talk only about their majors.
- And then an Internet "talk" request comes in from Zurich; it's "ksa," as Karim Saouli is known online, who manages the computer network for the math department of the Swiss Federal Institute of Technology. He's providing some key advice on our evolving computer network. We switch into "talk" mode; Karim's comments appear on the bottom half of my screen, while mine appear at the top. This is a very inexpensive mode of communication: $2 per hour between Zurich and Boston.
- Oops, better get moving, time's up; log off, and on to the phone.

Behind all this wonderful access and global connectivity lie some very big questions. The Internet, which erupted spontaneously and without great design, is growing up. It is being commercialized for the first time. The really big players are now deeply in the game: companies like IBM, MCI, Microsoft, and AT&T are forming new alliances among themselves daily. Government policy is being formulated in the roiling wash behind onrushing events. New security measures, both protective and intrusive, are being fiercely debated. And we're still a few years from the ultimate convergence of all digital technologies, the omnipresent pan-media/high-speed/full-spectrum bandwidth that will make everything available to everyone instantaneously all the time. Whew!

ALL THE WAY TO NEW YORK TO BUY A MODEM

When you take away all the technology, this vast, extended life space/ workplace comes back to people. How do people share ideas and resources in cyberspace? How do things get done? Who thinks about the whole? New leaders have arisen on the net, operating through influence and knowledge rather than through club, position, or legalities.

One such person is Lisa Kimball, who has been making her living catalyzing, coordinating, and cajoling networks for the past decade.

Lisa is an institution in the online community, "one of the early true believers in social transformation via networking," as Howard Rheingold describes her in *The Virtual Community.* "She practices what she preaches to the extent that it is hard to find any significant CMC [computer-mediated communication] system in the world that doesn't have a contribution from her."[13]

In 1984, Lisa became a partner in MetaSystems Design Group,[14] which runs MetaNet, short for The Meta Network, one of the oldest computer conferencing systems in the world, predating America Online by more than half a decade. In 1985, she founded the Electronic Networking Association in a loft in Greenwich Village, New York City; edited its award-winning online newsletter, *NETWEAVER*; chaired its annual meetings; received its 1990 award for "Outstanding Contribution to Networking"; and ultimately dismantled it when it had outlived its purpose. This is a key feature of networks; in essence, they are biodegradable. Unlike bureaucracies and hierarchies that often persist for years beyond their useful life, networks dissolve quickly when no longer needed.

"One of the advantages of the network structure is that groups can *dis*band as flexibly as they come together," she says. "Setting a 'sunset' date at the beginning prevents people from associating disbanding when 'done' with failure."

Lisa's iconoclastic, experience-worn view of organizational life spans both electronic and face-to-face milieus. When we published our *Networking Journal* in the mid-1980s, we asked Lisa to be our first guest columnist. In "A Networker's Diary," she took us along on her electronic adventures.

In 1994, she completed her Ph.D. in educational psychology at the Catholic University of America and is now moving faster than ever. For us, this chapter would not be complete without introducing Lisa. So, we sent an e-mail message requesting an interview. She was delighted and said that she was logging in from Michigan, where she was attending the Society for Human Ecology conference, "talking about participatory democracy." She asked for a list of questions and said she'd call later. By day's end, she was moving too fast to make a phone call. Instead, she replied online.[15]

LISA'S INTERVIEW

If there is ever a bumper sticker in her honor, it will say "Born to Network." Lisa started her career "in early elementary school," publishing a neighborhood newsletter "using lots of carbon paper." Her parents were her mentors. "My mother, Janet Fraser Kimball, worked downtown and seemed to know *everyone*." Her father, the journalist Penn Kimball, has a saying that inspires her: "There is no such thing as a boring person, only boring reporters."

Lisa's online life began in 1983, when she met Frank Burns, founder of The MetaNet. Another legend in the online world, Frank, a retired lieutenant colonel, is most famous for coming up with the Army recruiting line, "Be All That You Can Be."

Frank sat Lisa down "in front of [an] . . . old Kaypro, with its itty bitty screen, and told me what keys to hit.[16] The screen lit up, and I understood instantly that there were *people* in there (or out there . . . or *some*where) and I was totally thrilled."

But ill equipped. She lacked a modem and could only back-order one in the Washington, D.C., area. "So I went all the way to New York City to buy a 1200-baud Hayes internal modem for about $800, I recall . . . and I had to get extra memory because my 64K IBM with DOS 1.1 couldn't handle the modem," she says. It seems like a century ago.

For people like Lisa, the electronic world is not something separate from the rest of her life. "It's no more abstract than any other aspect of life," she says. "My life is rich with people I see in person, things I read online, people I interact with on networks, books I have stacked up next to my bed, relationships I maintain via telephone, electronic communities I am part of, my neighbors at our summer house, participants in this f-t-f [online-speak for face-to-face] conference, and participants in the online conference I'm attending now. The cyberspace world is merely another dimension of the world, with all of its complexities and beauty and mystery."

THE SOCIAL SCIENCES MEET NETWORKS

Profuse links are the defining characteristic of the Information Age. Links mean the physical connections *and* the relationships among the people. But:

Relationships, not technological connections, are the point.

We described thousands of grass-roots, voluntary organizations around the world that had little technology available to them in our first two books, *Networking* (1982) and *The Networking Book* (1986). Among these collectively powerful yet loosely structured associations, we detected the general principles that apply to all types of networks.

Since World War II, the words "network" and "networking" have emerged in virtually all the social sciences. From sociology and anthropology to psychology and psychiatry, from management and administrative sciences to city planning and infrastructure disciplines like communications, transportation, and waste treatment, networks carry an increasingly heavy conceptual load.

Virtually all uses of the word "network" in the sciences recognize "nodes," which we call "members," and "relationships," which we call "links," as their critical elements. Nearly all uses of the word in the human sciences also cite some variation on "shared purpose" as a basic criterion. Networks pervade social structure[17] and are understood in depth throughout a wide range of analytical tools developed primarily since the 1970s.[18]

People are always embedded in a web of social relationships, both personal and organizational. One major finding from multiple studies in Social Network Analysis is that the more complex people's webs are—that is, the greater the number of relationships they have—the happier and healthier they tend to be.[19] Particular cliques, groups, projects, and teamnets arise from the larger social network.

Rather than focusing on individual structures, regarding the greater network as a field of potential is of immense practical value. In this environment, the person who makes particular networks happen is the "coordinator."

"THE COORDINATOR," STARRING MRS. DEWAR

Coordinators appear everywhere in the Age of the Network, not just in new realms of cyberspace. Networks began developing new leaders long before computers enhanced their reach. In a richly connected environment where many potential projects are sparking, growing, diminishing, and disappearing, a new role arises, that of the coordinator, whose distinguishing characteristic is the ability to see "connections"[20] among people.

Elizabeth Meyer Lorentz will not receive the fame she deserves in her lifetime. Then again, she just might. As we write this, she is 81 and still networking.

With a small network that coalesced around the work of Yale psychology professor Seymour Sarason, Elizabeth has invented, commented on, and superbly played the role of the Coordinator. It has to be capitalized because it is so important. The network depends upon it. The Coordinator brings the network to life, matching needs with resources. It's a vital role, and Lorentz and company have been lending it legitimacy for nearly a quarter of a century. Elizabeth models coordinators after the role of the Oxford tutor, who "links students to the possibilities of the university and the world outside." Links. Possibilities.

Having just read Seymour's book, *The Creation of Settings and the Future Societies,*[21] she met him for lunch in the early 1970s at the Yale Faculty Club. "We were walking in the street when I said how great I thought his book was," she recalls. "Seymour stopped, turned, and said, 'Please don't be brief.' "[22] It was a good beginning to a long collaboration.

In their two books that followed, Elizabeth appears as the central character, Mrs. Dewar (pronounce it to understand it: "do-er"). As a trustee of her local hospital for more than 15 years, Elizabeth chaired the long-range planning committee. At the same time, Seymour and his colleagues had a federal grant to study networks. "Mrs. Dewar's network" became the object of their study, with her as the Coordinator Extraordinaire, involving the whole community, everyone who had a stake in the future of the hospital.

"I survived three executive and presidential changes," she recalls, "and I learned how the executives try to bypass the board. *They* were always plotting, so I'd plot back." Which she did by being a world-class coordinator.

"It's a radar type of mind that sees things and connections in the social fog that most people cannot," her peers reported. "I get lost trying to follow the connections she comes up with."[23]

"FINDING" PEOPLE

"The coordinator is a scanner of possibilities,"[24] Elizabeth says. To "design configurations of people," as she puts it, the coordinator must first "find" them.

So, Elizabeth invented a one-hour interview that usually turned into five. "They'd start canceling appointments left and right, and then I knew I was on track," she recalls. "The interviews help you 'find' the person."[25] "Finding" means identifying the person's full range of possibility, capability, skill, expertise, and talent. Elizabeth calls it "mapping a person's terrain, asset hunting instead of looking for what's wrong with people. A certain characteristic may be an asset, depending on what you match it with." She advises interviewers to:

- Think while you talk. Mentally match this person with others in the network. "Your job is to think, 'for whom is this an opportunity?' "[26]
- Make sure that the first vital phone call is made, even if you have to make it yourself for people who are reluctant.
- Get a real kick out of making a match; it's the coordinator's "reward. . . . An inner integration reflecting the outer one takes place," she says."
- Be ready to demean yourself and have no pride. "Like a little poodle, the coordinator has to gallop after people, asking their plans and reminding them by example that they are not a twosome but a part of a network."

Knowing the people in any network, not just in a community service one, is critical. Because it is a dynamic rather than a static organization, a network needs someone to coordinate the flow of people. No network survives without connections and coordination; for the techies, call it "gateways" and "network managers." It's all the same.

Yet, key practical questions remain unanswered. People will pay for technology network managers and infrastructure support, but will they pay for coordinators on the people side? Who trains them? How do you convince people that coordination is not an add-on to an existing job?

THE WORLD, WITH ALL OF ITS COMPLEXITIES AND BEAUTY AND MYSTERY

John Quarterman tracks the growth of global networking. What will happen he asks, when Marshall McLuhan's "global village," first described in his book by that name, is one of the largest countries on earth?[27] It's already larger than Australia and more than twice the size of Sweden, larger than Denmark, Ireland, Israel, and many countries in Africa combined. Never mind California. If Quarterman's projections are right, before long there will be more people using the Internet than citizens of any single country except India or China.

Perhaps. If commercialization of this precious resource is handled sensibly. If prices don't go sky high, so that use is expected to drop, as Australians now predict it will there.

"Only connect!" Links technological and social. With every connection, a little bit of good will is built, strengthening the social fabric, creating more trust.

CHAPTER 8

SOCIAL CAPITAL: NEW WEALTH BASED ON TRUST, RECIPROCITY, AND NETWORKS

When Digital Equipment Corporation started cutting costs in 1991, one of the first memos to come down from on high carried an ominous message. The company no longer would include in computer backups employees' "non-work-related" VAXNOTES files, the huge electronic conversation system that glued this global culture of 125,000 people together. Many lived their entire lives in NOTES, finding houses, spouses, consolation, job tips, and even recipes there. They also did their projects there, but these files would continue to be backed up. Unwittingly, Digital was cutting out the heart of its corporate trust system.

"Trust" is the short word that underlies successful transactions. Because people trust one another, they agree to work together. They make deals, undertake projects, set goals, and lend resources. Conversely, business grinds to a halt when trust breaks down.

Networks both need and generate trust. The more trust there is, the easier it is to do business. As trust accumulates—in teams, corporations, communities, and nations—it creates a new form of wealth. In the Age of the Network, *social capital* is as potent a source of wealth as land, resources, skills, and technology. To understand just how powerful an *economic* force social capital can be, we need to travel back in time nearly a millennium.

TWO PATHS, TWO SOCIETIES

As the curtain was lifting on the aptly named Dark Ages in Europe, Italy was in shambles. Throughout the peninsula, imperial rule had crumbled. Banditry was rampant. Restoring social order was the governmental imperative of the time. With the dawning of the 12th century, two radically different approaches emerged:

- In the south, steep vertical hierarchies rose up.
- In the north, horizontal networks spread out.

Hundreds of years later, these two paths reverberate still, not as faint echoes of the past but as powerful, pulsing shapers of the two disparate regions' cultures, institutions, and economies.

Beginning in the early 1100s, Italy's southern region fell under the organizing talents of Norman mercenaries. They superbly blended feudal autocracy and Byzantine bureaucracy. And for the next few centuries, they governed with relatively enlightened rule. Then, following the deaths of a line of great kings, prosperity began to wane. The steep hierarchy passed to the landed autocrats.

This vertical client–patron power structure remained intact throughout the next 800 years. In 1994, it is still spectacularly evident. The collapse of the central government through the corrosive action of corruption, a megascandal known as "Kickback City" (in Italian, *Tangentopoli*), was nearly a millennium in the making.

While the southern regimes of Roger II and Frederick II were early harbingers of the dominant Industrial Era structures, Italy's central and northern towns were remarkable forerunners of 21st-century organizational design.

COMMUNITY–STATES AND THE INVENTION OF CREDIT

Not since the rise of Athens and the other early Greek city-states had the West witnessed such a brilliant light of self-governance as shone in Florence, Venice, Bologna, Genoa, Milan, and other cities and towns in the north of Italy. From the 1100s, decentralized centers of communal republicanism rose and prospered. At their core were voluntary mutual-aid associations that neighbors formed for protection from marauding violence and economic cooperation.

> *"From the twelfth to the sixteenth century the feature which most distinguished Italian society from that in other regions in Europe was the extent to which men [sic] were able to take part in determining, largely by persuasion, the laws and decisions governing their lives."*[1]

People formed myriad mutual-aid groups in many spheres, creating a "rich network of associational life"—in neighborhoods, among parish priests and religious societies, in political parties, and within "tower societies" that provided security. Key among them were craft and trade guilds, formed for social as well as economic purposes. A "vivid sense of equality" coursed through the affairs of these communities.

Most remarkable was the economic creativity unleashed by the growing civic communities. The northern Italian republics invented *credit*, adding this fundamental tool to the already known classic economic factors of markets, money, and law.

Before the innovation of credit, private capital could accumulate but could not travel further in the economy. Credit links savings and investment. It enables economic growth, setting up an accumulating feedback loop whereby wealth can be used to create more wealth. The prosperity of the communal north flourished through finance and commerce, different from the affluence of the southern Sicilian Kingdom, where wealth was rooted in the land.

What lay at the heart of the discovery of credit a thousand years ago? Nothing more complex than an essential human quality already old by then—*trust*. Credit (from the word meaning "to believe") is possible only when there is mutual trust. In the *Oxford English Dictionary*, the third definition of credit *is* trust. The more trust exists, the more efficient credit is. The cost of mistrust goes down. With widespread trust in northern Italy:

> "[S]avings were activated for productive
> purposes to a degree inconceivable in previous
> centuries. . . . It was the widespread sense of
> honesty, strengthened by the sense of belonging
> to an integrated community, quite apart from
> definite legal obligations, which made possible
> the participation of all kinds of people with
> their savings in the productive process."[2]

Northern Italy has maintained a rich, concentrated culture built on extensive intertwined horizontal relationships throughout the centuries, through plagues, foreign occupations, and periodic impositions of client–patron controls.

EMILIA-ROMAGNA: THE REPRISE

An unexpected visitor arrived at our office in West Newton in late Fall, 1991. He had a message that he said we could not ignore in the book we were then writing. "You must tell the amazing story of what happens when many, many, small businesses form networks," said Jean-Pierre Pellegrin, a French official at the Organization for Economic and Cooperation and Development in Paris. "Emilia-Romagna, then Denmark. Write about them." "Them" turned out to be a very big story indeed, which begins in north central Italy.[3] The somewhat mysterious source of Emilia-Romagna's rags-to-riches story is the inspiration for the *flexible business network* movement throughout the world.

After a century of centralized rule from Rome, Italy decentralized in the 1970s. Emilia-Romagna ranked 18th in income among Italy's 21 administrative regions when these regions began to wrest autonomy from the central government.

Over the next decade, the economy exploded as hundreds of thousands of small businesses in Emilia-Romagna tied into networks. It had become the second wealthiest region in Italy, recording the greatest performance jump of any of the 80 European Community regions by the mid-1980s. Unemployment plunged from 20 percent to almost zero. By the late 1980s, there were 325,000 companies in this region of 4 million—an incredible ratio of 1 firm to 12 people, 90,000 of them in manufacturing.

Emilia-Romagna caught Denmark's attention. By the end of the 1980s, that country of 5 million, about the same size as Massachusetts, intentionally launched a similar effort. Denmark's success proved that many of the Italian lessons were transferable. In these two countries, government stimulated thousands of networks, positively affecting the national bottom line.

In the summer of 1993, Stuart Rosenfeld,[4] long a dedicated and articulate spokesman for flexible manufacturing networks, pointed us toward another startling dimension of the Italian story. A very-large-scale social science experiment, encompassing all of modern Italy beginning in 1970, richly documented the miracle of Emilia-Romagna.[5]

Italy's experience in moving from centralized to decentralized governance mirrors that of many organizations. Its mandate came long before its implementation. Italy's 1948 Constitution called for the nation to decentralize and establish administrative regions. But it took more than a generation for this to occur. Italy deliberately increased its number of bureaucratic pegs by establishing an entirely new level of government in 1970. With the regions came a set of governments with fairly equivalent roles, rules, and budgets.

> *This rare event in a developed democracy*
> *offered a natural experiment: a set of*
> *governmental constants and a wealth of social,*
> *cultural, and economic variables encompassing*
> *the many extremes represented in Italy.*

This extraordinary opportunity to do political *science* in the field was seized by Harvard professor of government Robert Putnam and a network of colleagues. Together they laid a baseline and tracked the ensuing institutional results. Putnam's book, *Making Democracy Work: Civic Traditions in Modern Italy*, succinctly summarizes their extensive findings and draws powerful implications for democracy and economic development.

They measured the performance of the new governments in three broad areas using 12 indicators:

- *Processes,* including cabinet stability, budget promptness, statistical and information services.
- *Law making,* including reform legislation and legislative innovation.
- *Implementation,* including day-care centers,[6] family clinics, industrial policy instruments, agricultural spending capacity, local health unit expenditures, housing and urban development, and bureaucratic responsiveness.

Perception is at least as important as reality in politics. These objective performance measures were tested against and found to be in close agreement with citizen and community leaders' opinions gathered by surveys and polls.

Amazingly, Emilia-Romagna topped the authors' "good government" charts[7] among all the regions. Why?

The Hunt for Civic Community

The quality of regional governments developed in dramatically different ways throughout Italy. Some regions were thriving, while others
were quagmired. These conclusions leaped out of the data—field
observations, case studies, quantitative techniques, and statistical
analysis—prompting the researchers to keep asking why. They like-
ned their search for clues to a detective mystery.

The usual explanation, that good socioeconomics leads to good
government, did not square with the data. Both the top performer and
the bottom one started in 1970 with many of the same below-average
social and economic indicators. Yet, Emilia-Romagna, in the north,
became the country's rising star, while Calabria, in the toe of Italy,
turned in the most dismal performance.

The answer, once they saw it, reverberated throughout the data:

- Indicators of good government[8] correlated with
- Places where people were joined in thick, overlapping networks,
  what the researchers termed "civic communities,"[9] which in turn
  mapped uncannily closely with the
- Most horizontally organized types of governments of the medieval states as they existed in 1300.[10]

"Civic communities" result when people engage in horizontal relationships "bound together by . . . reciprocity and cooperation," according to Putnam, rather than by vertical "authority and
dependency."[11] At the core of civic culture are two basic human
values—equality and trust. Civic societies are lush with social networks and associations of all sorts, an observation Alexis de Tocque-
ville made regarding the about-to-boom United States in his 1840
study, *Democracy in America*.

Many networks tightly braided people in Emilia-Romagna, which
had the top measures in both civic culture and institutional perfor-

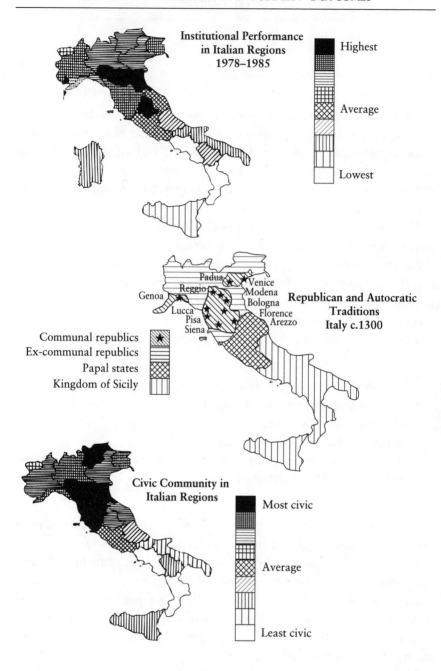

**Institutional Performance
in Italian Regions
1978–1985**

Highest

Average

Lowest

**Republican and Autocratic
Traditions
Italy c.1300**

Communal republics
Ex-communal republics
Papal states
Kingdom of Sicily

Padua
Venice
Reggio
Modena
Bologna
Genoa
Florence
Lucca
Arezzo
Pisa
Siena

**Civic Community in
Italian Regions**

Most civic

Average

Least civic

184

mance. Putnam calls it "the site of an unusual concentration of over-lapping networks of social solidarity, peopled by citizens with an unusually well developed public spirit—a web of civic communities. Emilia-Romagna is not populated by angels, but within its borders (and those of neighboring regions in north-central Italy) collective action of all sorts, including government, is facilitated by norms and networks of civic engagement."[12]

The results were simple and strong.
Governments were better where measures of
"civicness" were higher.

SOCIAL CAPITAL: THE 21ST CENTURY SOURCE OF WEALTH

Bologna, once the intellectual capital of the medieval communal republics, became the "new" regional capital of Emilia-Romagna in 1970.

What fueled the unprecedented economic growth there and the creation of excellent government? What resources of capital enabled such widespread creation of new wealth? Neither new land, natural resources, nor technology graced this ancient area. Not even human capital, meaning a highly educated and skilled populace, distinguished it.

What Emilia-Romagna did have in 1970 was an abundant stock of continuously renewing *social capital*.[13] Its wellspring of wealth had three tributaries:

- Trust,
- Reciprocity, and
- Dense social networks.

In the communal republics, extraordinary trust developed among myriad mutual-aid associations, enabling the civic regions of Italy to invent credit. The lesson of the past millennium applies immediately to today's flexible business networks.

"At the core of the mutual aid societies was practical reciprocity: I'll help you if you help me; let's face these problems together that none of us can face alone."[14]

Today these seats of Western civilization again have shown how to spin old relationships into new gold.

Relationships among the players lodge social capital. Unlike financial and human capital, social capital cannot be the property of individuals or corporations. By its very nature, it is jointly owned.

People generate wealth in dense networks of horizontal relationships in two primary ways:

- They lower transaction costs.
- They increase opportunities for productive cooperation.

Transactions are at the heart of business. All transactions, commercial and otherwise, particularly across boundaries and over time, embody trust. Transactions have costs—heaviest when trust is low, lightest where trust is high.

Mistrust is expensive. Informal communication goes down and formality goes up: endless forms and legalisms, time and effort spent checking other people's work, drawn out negotiations, political games and backstabbing, sticker-shock at the cost of third-party enforcement, corruption, and crime. When trust diminishes, price goes up.

"Scandals in fiduciary institutions dramatize the economics of trust," writes John O. Whitney in *The Trust Factor*. "During Drexel Lambert's last month before filing for Chapter 11, money hemorrhaged while the company's officers fought to restore credibility. In the spring of 1984, people lost confidence in Continental Bank of

Chicago. Money poured out. Very little new money came in. The bank had to be rescued. The savings and loan crisis wiped out the FSLIC. The epidemic of bank failures has almost wiped out the FDIC."[15]

Left unrenewed and unused, social capital runs down. It depletes, fragments, and dis-organizes with the wear and tear of transaction costs. Mistrust makes networks hard to form and relationships difficult to maintain, further diminishing trust—creating a vicious cycle. Unchecked, this social process searches for a stable state. In a dependent and exploitive culture held together by vertical controls, the norm becomes: "never cooperate."

But there is hope. Social capital also accumulates in virtuous cycles. Trust develops through *reciprocity* among people joined in *horizontal networks*. Reciprocity works in two ways as people:

- Barter in the here-and-now; and
- Bank benefits for the future, the barn-raising principle.

In barter, reciprocity is "balanced." There's an immediate and equivalent exchange, a trade of some kind (e.g., you pay the dry cleaner to get back your clothes). In barn-raising, reciprocity is "generalized," meaning "I'll do something today in the expectation of receiving some benefit from you, or others, in the future."

Future-oriented, barn-raising, cooperative behavior is the most productive type of reciprocity. It enables economic development.

"Rotating credit associations," a simple example found in virtually all cultures around the world, show how trust creates new wealth. Revolving loan funds—from villages in Bangladesh to Pine Ridge Reservation in South Dakota—happen when a group contributes a certain amount to a common pot. One member uses the collective pot, perhaps to increase his or her productivity (e.g., to buy seed or a plow). After receiving the benefit, members, of course, continue to contribute. Why "of course"? Because in dense networks, where people know one another well, the cost of lost opportunities and the threat of ostracism are prohibitive.

Trust lowers the cost of cooperation and deposits money in the bank. Informal communication increases, while formalities decrease and the need for paperwork recedes. Negotiations are brief and conclusive, while the need for "checkers" evaporates as people spend time in "real work" rather than supervision because all persons involved simply keep their word. Social capital accumulates with trust and reciprocal relationships. It remains scattered and unformed without trust. People generate trust through their interpersonal networks of relationships.

OPEN AND CLOSED LOGICS OF COOPERATION

"Greed, mismanagement ravage fisheries," reads the 1994 headline.[16] Near us, both the United States and Canada are invoking drastic measures to curtail the catch on the once rich Georges Bank fishing grounds off the New England and Newfoundland coasts. Local economies are devastated. A precious resource is in dire danger globally.

Georges Bank is a real-world example of "the tragedy of the commons," whereby people ruin a common area by overuse. When unlimited economic actors maximize their individual gain by exploiting a shared resource, they destroy a natural, shared source of wealth. Add continuously improving technology, such as in ocean fishing, and the spiral to exhaustion accelerates.

This "dilemma of collective action," as it is known in game theory, is one of several logical puzzles that suggest that cooperation is either folly or, at best, a rarely rational choice. Early game theorists made the science of economics more dismal than Malthus had ever done with such thinking. The winning strategy, in closed cycles of transactions and isolated games played once, is to "get as much as you can and never cooperate." Selfishness is logical and rational.

However, when people play repeated games, the logic changes dramatically. People become more cooperative when their behavior in one transaction carries forward to subsequent ones. In "infinitely repeated games," cooperation suddenly becomes rational and practical, according to more recent game theory studies.[17]

Game theory predicts, and Putnam's study demonstrates, that society holds together at two "quite different levels of efficiency and institutional performance." In one case, the informing principle is to "always defect." In the other, the motto is to "reciprocate help."

These self-reinforcing dynamics, reciprocity–trust and dependence–exploitation, reflect building up and tearing down. They are, respectively, "vicious" and "virtuous" loops, amplifying through positive feedback.[18]

- *Vicious*: In isolated situations where there are no consequences in the future and relationships are top-down, people "never cooperate," a predictable, suspicious, stable state. It's safer and more "rational" to "always defect," to be mistrustful and exploitive.
- *Virtuous*: When the players connect in rich networks, "brave reciprocity" prevails. News about trustworthy and untrustworthy behavior spreads quickly and widely. Here the norm is different: "Cooperate with people who cooperate with you (or who cooperate with people like you), and don't be the first to defect."[19]

Trust, reciprocity, and networks all are mutually reinforcing, whether on the rise or on the wane.

> *Trust is at the personal core; reciprocity is at*
> *the interface; and networks tie it all together.*

Networks facilitate communication and extend trust. When success spreads through a network, it stimulates more cooperation, providing models for others about what works. Innovation increases as the latest information and trends create a large-scale learning system in which many potential users share knowledge.

Innovation is stunning among Emilia-Romagna's hundreds of thousands of tiny, networked companies. As so many have observed about this region, it reflects a vital dynamic that simultaneously integrates vigorous competition *and* cooperation—co-opetition—among many independent players.[20]

These lessons have a timeless quality. They apply both on grand scales and on intimate ones.

NEW WORLD REGIONAL ADVANTAGE

Imagine what higher levels of trust mean in your organization—with suppliers, customers, competitors, regulators, and special interests. Picture the regional advantage that accrues from a high-trust community.[21]

While Putnam and his colleagues were scrutinizing the Old World, AnnaLee Saxenian, a professor of city and regional planning at the University of California at Berkeley, was examining two distinct industrial regions in the New World: Route 128 on the colonial coast of Massachusetts and Silicon Valley in north central California.

The booming computer revolution of the 1970s produced two star regions of great innovation and explosive entrepreneurial growth. By the early 1980s, the semiconductor business that had fueled Silicon Valley seemed to be slipping westward to Japan. In the east around the Boston "Hub," minicomputers, which had broken the stranglehold of mainframes, now faced their great challenge: individual workstations and the runaway success of personal computers.

Both regions plunged into recession. One bounced back. Silicon Valley is lush territory again in the global economic ecology of the mid-1990s. Even though Massachusetts' economy as a whole is doing better than California's, the computer companies that powered the Massachusetts Miracle continue to slump and retrench.

TWO REGIONAL BUSINESS CULTURES

The reason is clear, says Saxenian. "Distinct industrial systems" developed in these regions after World War II. She compares them [bullets added]:

Silicon Valley has a regional-network-based industrial system—that is, it promotes collective learning and flexible adjustment among companies that make specialty products within a broad range of related technologies.

• The region's dense social networks and open labor market encourage entrepreneurship and experimentation.
• Companies compete intensely while learning from one another about changing markets and technologies through informal communication and collaboration.
• . . . The organizational boundaries within companies are porous, as are the boundaries between companies themselves and between companies and local institutions such as trade associations and universities.

The Route 128 region is dominated by a small number of relatively vertically integrated corporations.

• Its industrial system is based on independent companies that keep largely to themselves.
• Secrecy and corporate loyalty govern relations between companies and their customers, suppliers, and competitors, reinforcing a regional culture that encourages stability and self-reliance. Corporate hierarchies ensure that authority remains centralized, and information tends to flow vertically.
• The boundaries between and within companies, and between companies and local institutions, thus remain distinct in the independent-company-based system.[22]

It's all relative. Route 128 is not Calabria in southern Italy. Nor does Silicon Valley have 800 years of cooperative history behind it. Yet the differences between vertical and horizontal business cultures are distinctive and highly instructive.

CORPORATE COMPARISONS

There are many micro corporate stories within the macro East–West regional story. Saxenian compares Apollo Computer and Sun Microsystems. Apollo virtually created the workstation market in 1980 with a superior technology and a two-year lead on Sun. But by 1987, Apollo had permanently fallen behind the faster, more flexible Sun. Two years later, Hewlett-Packard bought Apollo.

Apollo created insular, self-reliant, vertically integrated, proprietary operating systems for its machines that mirrored the nature of its organization. In contrast, Sun adopted an open operating system, Unix, from the beginning, and an open way of doing business that used standard components from vendors while rapidly introducing new products.

Saxenian also contrasts the computer systems giants in each region, Hewlett-Packard (H-P) and Digital Equipment Corporation (DEC). The comparison is particularly meaningful to us since we spent eight years—1985 to 1992—as independent consultants doing work for DEC and its customers in organizational networks.

Both H-P and DEC had $13 billion in revenues in 1990. Both of their proprietary computer systems were under siege from the fast-paced challenges of systems opening everywhere in hardware, operating systems, and applications. What was their response? Saxenian said:

- Hewlett-Packard gradually opened itself by building a network of local alliances and sub-contracting relationships, while strengthening its global reach.
- DEC, in spite of its formal commitment to decentralization, retained a substantially more self-sufficient organizational structure and corporate mind-set.[23]

From the beginning, H-P's founders, William Hewlett and David Packard, sought to avoid the hierarchical structures of the East Coast. The " 'H-P Way' . . . includes a participative management style that supports, even demands, individual freedom and initiative while emphasizing commonness of purpose and teamwork."[24] H-P leveraged management "by wandering around," by paying attention to physical settings to encourage informal communications, and by the "elimination of most traditional corporate symbols of hierarchy and status, including private offices, reserved parking spaces, and differentiated attire and office furniture."

DEC, too, sought to organize differently from traditional East Coast corporations. Its founder, Ken Olsen, also "pioneered a management model based on organizational decentralization and a participatory culture."[25] The resulting matrix organization, crossing product lines and functions, was once regarded as a model of advanced management. But, says Saxenian, "the matrix structure also masked extensive centralization: it allowed Olsen and a small number of powerful senior committees that survived the company's frequent reorganizations to retain final authority for all important decisions."[26] The principles of openness and debate all too often degenerated into vicious internal conflict.

Intense rivalries existed within and among the vice presidential units of the company. Project conflicts were known by such names as "The Database Wars" and bureaucracy ballooned. Even with consistent, long-term contractors, DEC resisted umbrella purchase orders. Each new bit of work required its own paperwork; it could take as many as 19 steps to get an invoice paid.

In 1994, H-P was flourishing and DEC's struggle continued, losing money and employees. Silicon Valley illustrates something different. A regional culture of dense networks offers a competitive advantage to big companies as well as small ones, to older companies as well as startups.

Trust also turns into value *within* organizations, as Eastman Chemical Company's story shows. It demonstrates some ways to increase the stock of social capital.

EASTMAN'S PATH TO HIGHER TRUST

When Bob Joines, Eastman's vice president of quality (see chapter 3), spoke with us in 1994, trust was on his mind. His first remark was about trust, and he threaded it throughout the whole exchange.

"We have been working on teams for many years," said Joines. "We realized that unless we removed some social impediments and barriers to trust, teams would not be effective."

"Ask what the trust level is," Joines advises other firms. "When you find out it's not as high as you want, then you need to examine why. Look into the company's substructure and define the impediments to trust."

In 1985, Eastman began their look, inaugurating a process of change that eventually reorganized a vertical culture into a horizontal one. They discovered that mistrust was built into their systems. To build trust, they had to:

- trash the traditional performance system;
- throw out the time-honored, 70-year-old suggestion system;
- equalize perks and symbols; and, most astonishingly,
- question team rewards.

"WE JUST SAID NO"

It started with the way people got paid. "We hire the 'best and the brightest' from college, the 3.8s, 3.9s, 4.0 grade point averages, people at the top of their classes," Joines remarked. "Then we say in our performance system that half of you are below average and that we are going to reward you accordingly. Now, everybody get your heart and mind engaged and be an owner of the enterprise.

"We interviewed 1,500 people over a six-month period. In the end, we just said no to our performance system and stopped it. There was an amazing, fantastic ground swell of opinion to scrap it.

"We didn't know how to solve the pay problem, but we knew enough to push the decision down in the organization. Budgets give a pot of personnel money to a unit and let the unit determine how to allocate it.

"We try to articulate principles with which to make decisions rather than give prescriptions." Here Joines again emphasized the importance of providing learning and theory, as well as training and skills, to manage hot issues like money and performance evaluation.

Another pillar of Eastman's culture proved to be an unlikely impediment to teamwork. Seventy years ago, George Eastman, the company's founder, established the suggestion system: if you have a good idea, get a suggestion form, fill it out, and get rewarded financially, up to $25,000.

"Look at the logic," Joines said analytically. "If I have a great idea, why should I share it with my teammates or anyone else? So we just said no to our suggestion system. It's demeaning to say that the company regularly pays for your hands and feet but not your head. Park your brain in your car? *No.* We want the feet, hands, *and* brains of everyone, all the time."

LITTLE THINGS COUNT

Eastman knew that they couldn't build trust simply by rebricking one or two major systems. Here the devil was in the details, in the small, seemingly insignificant things that affect people on a daily basis. Benefits such as health and vacations varied widely, with options graded from the executive suite to the shop floor. Now benefits options are the same for everyone.

"We changed the dress code and parking privileges, closed the executive dining room, and opened a business dining room. These things seem trivial, but they involve important issues of trust and the perception of trust. We need people to feel like owners of our enterprise."

We were surprised to learn that Eastman had virtually stopped giving special rewards to teams. This appears to run counter to what most teams have been striving for.

"Who's the team?" Joines questioned. "We ask a production unit that exceeds its goals, 'Are the people who provided maintenance for you part of the team? How about purchasing people who made your JIT deliveries possible? Or the cafeteria staff who provided extra meals so you could continue working?' So we've backed away from using team compensation, which tends to drive a wedge between teams. The company becomes the team.

"We're still learning. We don't have the issues worked out or fine-tuned. But the philosophy is in the hands of the people who have to administer it, not in a central function."

From medieval communal republics to a new high-tech region to an old company with a new vitality, trust is the key.

ISLANDS OF TRUST

There are "islands of trust" at every scale. Couples, partners, families, groups, neighborhoods, departments, communities, enterprises, regions, industries, and nations all have stocks of social capital. Company cultures are storage vaults of social capital based on their history and current dynamics. This investment is available to capitalize (or not) new relationships. Each time a new group comes together, it plants the seed for a new island of trust.

WHEN THE VELOCITY OF TRUST ACCELERATES

Social capital basically consists of information about relationships among people. It doesn't behave in quite the same way as physical capital. Matter, when used, degrades. Information, when used, accumulates. Unused, information loses value or becomes a weapon in the struggle to compete and control, increasing mistrust. Like communication, trust is very personal and yet cannot be possessed by a single individual. It takes at least two to trust.

Trust, or its lack, is an all-pervasive cross-cultural reality. All people in all cultures in all ages have depended on trust, but its value greatly expands in the Age of the Network.

- Trust enables *links* to be constructed. It undergirds the high-performing organization with the profuse voluntary communications of fast, flexible, integrated responses.
- If purpose is the glue, trust is the grease. *Purposes* operate through trust—the source of legitimacy for and the vital spark of networks. Trust enables people to establish purposes articulated in detail and maintained over time.

The greater the trust, the lower the cost of communication and relationship building. The more extensive the network, the greater the opportunities arising from commonly held goals.

Conversely, mistrust creates difficulties at each step in developing a purpose. It takes longer to arrive at common goals since suspicion demands greater specificity. Enforcement is costly in terms of legal, accounting, and inspection fees and close monitoring is burdensome, sometimes proving fatally inflexible to change.

Among the ebbs and flows of turbulence and quiet come some defining moments—usually unexpected and often unwelcome. Crises often precipitate positive feedback loops in social capital—either viciously or virtuously. The vast 1993 Mississippi River floods, for example, drew upon and reinforced the hard-won prairie values of neighborly help at the same time that half of the Cabinet and President Clinton flew to the Midwest to coordinate the federal government's response. Awful as the rising water was, the flood also washed in new wealth through social capital formed by countless helping hands as some compensation for the damage.

In the Age of the Network, social capital is continuously being formed or degraded. It increases and decreases through dynamics fed by history, circumstances, crises, and creativity.

*In the Age of the Network, horizontal
connections explode, not vertical ones. The
winners in the 21st century—companies,
countries, and people—will be those with the
greatest social capital.*

All islands of trust, large or small, are embedded in larger environments of relationships that themselves represent stocks of social capital. Social fabrics can be rent by disasters—natural and otherwise, from the Valdez oil spill to Chernobyl to Hurricane Andrew—that threaten the health of communities and families; by migrations and refugees; and by rippling layoffs that destroy economic and personal stability. Relationships are difficult to maintain as physical infrastructures deteriorate, inhibiting travel and communication. Poverty creates isolation, dependence, and lack of access to connections. Most corrosively, reaching into all communities, violence and fear undermine and attack this form of social wealth.

The key to a society's ability to generate social capital lies in its practice of equality—political, social, and economic. Equality is under siege by the powerful global trend of an evolving two-class society, 20 percent wealthy and 80 percent poor, both within and among nations.[27]

This widening disparity will have to be reversed for the benefits of cooperation to be reaped on a global scale. To do so, John Evans, chairman of Torstar, the parent company of Canada's largest newspaper, *The Toronto Star*, says, we need "a new investment of social capital in community [and] new networks of civic engagements, involvements and commitments from individuals, private groups, corporations. . . . 'A society that relies on generalized reciprocity and mutual assistance is more effective than a competitive, distrustful society.' "[28]

A MATTER OF SURVIVAL

Ross Ashby's "Law of Requisite Variety"[29] is one of the most famous systems principles. In essence, the law says that for a system to survive, it needs to be at least as complex as its environment. As the environment becomes more complex, the system—whether an organism or an organization—learns and adapts, handling more complexity. Otherwise, sooner or later it dies.

As our world becomes more complex, accelerates, and swells more global, we need to smarten up. Growing smarter means incorporating more variety, gaining access to what's happening, and intelligently connecting bits of knowledge to anticipate the future. As the pace speeds up, organizations must incorporate even greater diversity to survive and thrive. More complexity compels more organizations to develop network strategies and paths of change to increase their social capital.

Networks incorporate diversity and carry reciprocity across boundaries and borders of every scale and scope. Wide-ranging webs provide the amplifying effect that social network analyst Mark Granovetter calls "the strength of weak ties."[30] He shows how connections at the edges of people's networks, rather than conversations in their core cliques, boost the effects of innovations, ideas, and opportunities.[31]

Boundary-crossing networks decrease the cost of transactions and open new channels of cooperation over which new patterns of trust develop.

Apple, IBM, and Motorola astonished many when they announced their joint venture to develop a new computer chip. Just a few years earlier, Apple and IBM, for example, were mortal enemies. By the time the project was well underway, the three companies even opened their e-mail systems to one another.

Boundary-crossing networks expand social capital.

Teamnets provide extra value beyond accomplishing specific goals like developing a new chip. By bringing people together to pursue shared aims, they add to the stock of social capital. Even when people participate in networks that fail, they frame new relationships and bank trust that they can draw upon in the future.

THE BIOLOGICAL INTERNET

"Trust is really essential," Frank Starmer says (see chapter 1 for more information on his global "lab without walls"). For a group to be creative, it must have trust. Islands of trust do not have to be vast to be vital.

"It's essential to develop a level of trust where you can say anything and not regret it or feel that it will come back to haunt you," Frank says. "Only then are all the communication paths open. No one is wasting time trying to decide whether to say this or that. Complete openness and freedom lead to unconstrained thinking, which leads to good science or good art or good whatever you're doing.

"Collectively, we feel stronger as a team than we do as individuals. Otherwise, we'd drop out of the group. There'd be nothing to gain. Together, we are more competitive in the science world. Each person contributes some special talent or insight into our overlapping interests."

"We speak of a biological Internet. Each person has a nervous system that coordinates and controls. But there is also absolute trust between every part of the body. It's essential for coordinated behavior. And our lab without walls is just a big collective organism with a common goal."

Imagine your organization with that level of trust. Common goals, coordinated effort, unconstrained thinking, each person contributing, more competitive, all-channel open communication—and the creative juices are really flowing. Trust is the key to success.

SECTION V

LOOKING AHEAD

CHAPTER 9

NETWORKING TRENDS: A WINDOW TO THE FUTURE

FROM HIERARCHY-BUREAUCRACY TO TEAM-NETWORKS

There is nothing elegant about their conference room. It is plain, neon lighted, and windowless; the furniture looks like government issue. Situated in the high-security manufacturing center for "plastics," AT&T Universal Card Services' GetNet team is having its launch meeting. The purpose of GetNet is to aggressively increase receivables by the end of the next fiscal year, a goal set by the company's CEO, David Hunt.

Now Hunt is standing in front of some 30 members of the cross-organizational team tasked with making GetNet happen—vice presidents, managers, and associates.

"What worked a year ago won't work today," Hunt says, wearing a blue shirt, no jacket, and a red, white, and blue tie. "We have to be able to change midstream. The environment is changing, and it will change again. Adaptability and flexibility are key in the marketplace."

Hunt's job is to shepherd a young 1990 startup, born out of a very old company, into the 21st century. "Change" is the most prominent feature on his horizon; he uses the word three times in four sentences.

To a credit card company like this one, change means interest rates

203

that spike and slump, intense competition from a crowded field of providers, upstart offers that take them by surprise, and the constant threat of a breakdown that could destroy a whole "vintage," the industry term for a mass mailing of millions of pieces.

So AT&T Universal Card Services, one of AT&T's 22 subsidiaries, a 1992 Malcolm Baldrige National Quality Award winner, pushes ahead. Besides its projected revenue goal, it is trying to raise its quality score another 100 points on the Baldrige scale, from 800 to 900 (1,000 is tops). This is virtually unheard of. It is reengineering its major business processes. Scores of teams populate the company; the senior executive level is known simply as the "B-Team" (B as in business). And, thanks to the efforts of Mike Plummer, an energetic internal consultant, the company is forging "learning partnerships to move to the next frontier of employee involvement."[1]

METATRENDS: CURRENTS OF CHANGE

Like its competitors, AT&T Universal Card lives in the Age of the Network. It must guard against using the default organization, 19th-century hierarchy-bureaucracy, in place of 21st-century team-networks to continue to be successful. This *meta*trend toward networks is so fundamental that it permeates all human organizations and embraces us all daily.

Everywhere around us, networks occur organically in nature as well as in human affairs. You see them referred to in the paper and on the air, concerning life at home, at work, in the community, and among nations. Notice how frequently you hear the word "network" and use it yourself. Check how often the idea—wherever it appears—expresses one or more of the five teamnet principles. Judge whether this metatrend appears in the areas of the world you know and care about.

The outburst of networked organizations is not the only force propelling us into the Information Age, but it is on the short list.[2] Overlapping, cross-cutting fundamental trends include:

- exploding information and its technology;
- economies that globalize and localize at the same time;
- complexity without rival in human history; and, as Hunt says,
- the high-velocity, accelerating pace of change.

Grouped, these powerful metatrends shape an infinite variety of unique events and patterns that make up everyday life.

Today we are well into the transition from the Industrial Age to the Information Age. More important, we are way past startup and, for the most part, beyond the moment of launch in the Information Age life cycle.

Organizational structures are crackling with the combustion of change. Every organization is changing somewhere, somehow. Structures and processes that are "decentralized," "flat," "horizontal," "teamed," "allied," and "virtual" are realities, not the stuff of future predictions.

We live the future, but only in part. Most of us are caught in situations that are betwixt and between.

TERRA FIRMA MEETS THE UNPREDICTABLE FUTURE

We straddle two ages. Mainstream approaches to organizational change stand with one foot in the predictable past, the other seeking *terra firma* in a radically unpredictable future.

Three broad initiatives comprise much of the current best thinking on how to transform organizations:

- Quality,
- Reengineering,
- Teams.

All three areas involve numerous companies. With its beginnings in the 1980s for many U.S. companies, quality today often is institutionalized, either in a function and/or through training. New companies don't even think of organizing without including a quality component.

Reengineering, particularly hot in 1994 with the publication of *Reengineering the Corporation* by Michael Hammer and James Champy,[3] likely is afoot in most organizations (even if only in the talking stage).

In the wake of both efforts, teams mushroom everywhere.

Although quality no longer seems new, it has set a new organizational baseline. Marriott's motto stretches over the doorway of its hotels: "Every guest leaves satisfied." We wondered whether this was just a slogan when we first saw the banner in a Jacksonville, Florida, Marriott. It proved accurate for us. When we needed breakfast before the kitchen opened, we got it by special arrangement to fit our schedule.

A promise to guests, but also a challenge to competitors. Hyatt and Sheraton read this and have to wonder whether their properties would do the same. Even Marriott has to be concerned about just how common our experience is. Your company's products and processes are constantly tested and forced to higher levels of performance by competitors who are increasing quality and decreasing costs. This miracle happens when you do more with less, a tangible result of an applied organizational advantage.

Reengineering and quality share several characteristics. Both use the same systems model. With their vigorous process orientation, both also emphasize the importance of purpose and use customers as a focus in finding it. They also differ fundamentally, in a classic East–West sort of way, which is what makes them so useful together.

- Quality is about continuous improvement.
- Reengineering is about radical, dramatic breakthroughs in organizational performance. To achieve sharply greater performance, reengineering relies heavily on information technology.

Reengineering is a perfect age-spanning concept. The term itself suggests bolts and wrenches, the mechanism of the passing Industrial Age. To "re"-"engineer" some "thing," you first must have built it. Yet reengineering catapults its way into the next century with its clear focus on process and its close alliance with information technology.

Teams stretch even further back across the ages, reaching to the Nomadic Age, when people first acquired small-group skills. The best teams rediscover and reaffirm ancient knowledge of how a small group can work together for mutual advantage.

Both quality and reengineering generate teams, often multiple ones. Teams of innovators get these programs and pilots going—decision makers, developers, trainers, and users. Then implementations beget teams, sometimes hundreds of them in very large companies.

Eastman's 18,000 employees now work in 800–900 vertical interlocking teams and 500–600 horizontally linked, cross-functional teams, a trend that began with its first quality initiative. Reengineering regularly requires teams—both to design the new processes and to implement them.

Our experience in working on a reengineering project at an international airline is typical. A core team of about seven redesigned the planning of the carrier's schedules, with input from dozens of others. Ultimately, hundreds of people throughout the company would have participated in "a network of business development teams." But like many reengineering efforts, this one remained essentially on the drawing boards two years after it was proposed, having fallen victim to competing priorities—downsizing, merger, new management, and new investors.

Teams also are a natural reaction to crises of every sort, being used to carry out special projects and to solve large, general problems. Asea Brown Boveri's Swedish software company, ABB Network Control, set up 20 teams of 15 people each (see chapter 5) when they wanted to become a learning organization. The energetic, deliberately diversely populated teams arrived at their "Life-Long Learning" solution within a few months.

Teams are central to the systems approach to management, especially the social-technical methods, which address both the design of the organization and the technology. A "team organization" is also a strategy in itself, with a large number of current management books devoted to the topic attesting to its power.

Teams share the emphasis on purpose that characterizes both quality and reengineering. Virtually all team literature emphasizes the importance of establishing a unifying purpose, this definition in *The Wisdom of Teams* being typical:

"A team is a small number of people with complementary skills who are committed to a common purpose, performance goals, and approach for which they hold themselves mutually accountable."[4]

The "small number"—somewhere between a minimum of two and a maximum of two dozen—is not an incidental constraint. To be effective, everyone on the team needs to know everyone else well.

But teams are not always the solution. All too often, management sets up teams as a knee-jerk reaction, a syndrome that Geri Lincoln, a quality expert at the U.S. Postal Service, has dubbed HAMFAT— "Have A Meeting, Form A Team." The automatic appointment of a random team then contributes to the problem.

Repeatedly, teams become isolated. They feed the fragmentation problem when they are not part of an overall organizational design and strategy. In addition, many patterns of teamwork—close partnerships, intimate relationships, instantaneous hand-offs—do not work easily beyond the limits of a small group. Companies that boast "teams" of 500 or even 1,000 are not really talking about teams. This is not to say that teams do not appear at every level—from the shop floor to the executive suite.

When joined into networks, however, teams have the ability to grow large. While the size of each team remains small, the bounds of the network as a whole can be quite grand.

LEARNING ORGANIZATIONS

The "learning organization" is another major movement now rising on many management agendas. Most broadly, this term embraces how groups and people use and process information, converting it into knowledge and, in the best situations, into wisdom. It sits squarely in the Information Age.

The great management theorist Peter Drucker first used the term "knowledge worker" as early as 1950. For almost a half century, Drucker has been pointing to a radical change in the nature of work: people who deal primarily with information are the expanding ranks of labor, having decades ago eclipsed factory workers, just as those on the assembly line once replaced farm labor. Knowledge, according to Drucker, is now the dominant form of capital in the Information Age economy.

Peter Senge's 1990 instant classic, *The Fifth Discipline: The Art & Practice of the Learning Organization*, brought the learning organization to management's permanent attention. It's a very appealing concept. Senge defines learning organizations as places "where people continually expand their capacity to create the results they truly desire, where new and expansive patterns of thinking are nurtured, where collective aspiration is set free, and where people are continually learning how to learn together."[5] A learning organization requires five core disciplines, according to Senge, a set strongly suggestive of teamnets:

- Personal mastery,
- Mental models,
- Shared vision,
- Team learning, and, the fifth discipline,
- Systems thinking.

Focus on the learning organization will grow, and the implications will deepen. The idea that human organizations have "cognitive capabilities," meaning that they are able to think in some meaningful human sense, will become mainstream. Corporate memory, reasoning, decision making, and creativity all become more visible in the learning organization.

The intelligence of a network lies in the pattern of relationships among its members. It is the "more than" that interacting parts create in forming a whole. The analogy to the physical pattern of a biological neural net is irresistible.

Saab is not the only company to proclaim "intelligence" as a feature of its product. Other ads that tout a company as being "smart" suggest that an organization as a whole really does think. Hype becomes reality as the Age of Information and the Network continues to mature.

Learning is *an* essential, if not *the* essential, skill for adapting to change for organizations as well as people.

"CREATE CONSTANCY OF PURPOSE"

Quality, reengineering, teams, and learning all contribute to organizational change in the 1990s. Networks complement and enhance these approaches rather than replace them. Networking is an integrative philosophy, one that seeks commonalities and contact among many conceptual islands.

- "Create constancy of purpose," W. Edwards Deming, the father of quality, said in the first of his famous "14 Points" for quality improvement. Unified purpose is central to quality, reengineering, teams, learning, *and* networks. Indeed, it is the source of legitimacy in the Age of the Network, quite different from the tradition that ruled the nomads, the coercive force that has reigned in hierarchy, and the supreme laws that govern bureaucracy.
- Networks comprise diverse types of organizations. Hierarchies and bureaucracies can be independent, self-organized, self-reliant network members. Bureaucratic boxes can add value to a net-

work, not as isolated functional units but as independent integrated elements of the whole.

- The "big news" about networks is links, both physical and relationships humane. The technology for communication has never been more plentiful—and it's growing. At the same time, people are looking carefully at horizontal processes to design work. The horizontal view becomes ever more vital as time drives work and change challenges it. People will value relationships increasingly for their store of social capital and learning.
- Traditional "one-'man'-at-the-top" leadership is under challenge by all the change movements. Multiple leadership—where more than one person has responsibility for outcomes—requires appointed and natural leaders, social and task leaders, bosses and coaches, and experts of all sorts, as well as new roles such as that of coordinator. It also means that some people will have to give up power. At the same time, the fundamental global change in the work force infuses rich, new styles of leadership as women and minorities slowly but inexorably ascend the ladder of power.
- Networks scale. They are multilevel structures—hierarchies in the generic sense of the word—that provide vertical alignment. From the top down comes guidance for the work processes, which are for the most part horizontal.[6]

Networks tie teams together into robust yet rapidly changing learning structures. Cross-boundary management of reengineered processes leads to a more flexible, horizontal organization. "Continuous improvement involving everyone," called *kaizen* in Japan, and the systematic removal of barriers to teamwork push quality organizations naturally toward team*nets*.

Networks offer a clear vision of the future organization at work today, including and going beyond teams, hierarchies, and bureaucracies.

VISIONS OF TWO WORLDS

"Adopt the new philosophy," said Deming in the second of his 14 Points.[7] In his fifth point, he said, "We are in a new economic age. Improve constantly and forever the system of production and service, to improve quality and productivity, and thus constantly decrease costs." This is the heart of continuous improvement. Doing more can cost less? How can this be?

> *Relationships that increase trust, reciprocity, and participation in networks generate new wealth beyond their immediate productive results.*

It seems to us that Deming's vision of quality inherently includes the idea of social capital (see chapter 8), the nonmonetary source of wealth that lowers the cost of cooperation. What Deming had called for is quite simply "civic community in the workplace."

Most of his 14 Points are directed toward removing barriers to teamwork and building social capital:

- Cease dependence on inspection;
- Don't award business based on price alone. Build a long-term relationship of loyalty and trust with your suppliers;
- Train on the job;
- Institute leadership;
- Drive out fear;
- Break down barriers between departments;
- Eliminate slogans, exhortations, and targets;
- Substitute leadership for work standards and management by numbers;
- Remove barriers that rob the employees of the right to pride of workmanship;

- Institute a vigorous program of education and self-improvement; and, finally,
- Put everyone in the company to work to accomplish the transformation. The transformation is everyone's job.

On a flight from Atlanta to New Orleans, another passenger struck up a conversation. He was shocked to learn that we understood his work, process improvement (in a sporting goods conglomerate), that we'd even heard of it. We said we did something similar. He did not agree. There is no process improvement without the numbers, he argued. All the "team stuff is useless," he said.

Many companies have failed to achieve the benefits of quality because they cannot achieve them with the numbers alone. True quality requires heart, cross-boundary trust, and long-term relationships—the actual sources of new wealth.

In the logic of game theory, interactions stabilize around one of two stances: either "never cooperate," a "vicious" vertical one, or "brave reciprocity," the "virtuous" horizontal one. If you aren't on the virtuous path, enlarging social capital, you're probably careening down its opposite, the vicious route, where social capital is declining.

Brave reciprocity is an appealing ideal. It enhances the quality of life, inspires high performance, and has just enough risk to keep things interesting. Bob Joines of Eastman spoke of the deeper Deming, the man who "talks about joy in the work." "Joy," said Joines, "this is the importance of working together."

NAVIGATING RAPID CHANGE

Transitions are tough—predictably so. You need good vision and sharp intelligence to navigate rapid change. You also need good models. Here are some 21st-century trends that appear when you tune in to the frequencies of the future using the network model, grouped according to the five teamnet principles.

SHIFTS IN PURPOSE

Trends focused on purpose, the first of the five principles, set the stage for the 21st-century organization.

> • *Radical change will prevail for the foreseeable future. Organizations will either create their own futures or find themselves reacting to the future that is controlling them.*

To get where you want to go, you need vision. Successful proactive behavior requires enormous flexibility coupled with a clear view of where you are going.

Theory is particularly useful in cross-boundary contexts. It provides guidelines and tools for local use rather than prescriptions. By making explicit the basic assumptions and models behind your vision, you can treat them as hypotheses. Then you can test and improve them through experience.

> *Emphasis is shifting from managing "costs" to focusing on real business growth.*

Many, if not most, quality and reengineering efforts are directed at cutting costs. Numberless *ad hoc* teams have been set up to do the same thing. Yet many organizations, if not industries, have already squeezed out most excess costs. The question is, what's next?

There is an alternative to downsizing: expand the business. Here big business can learn from the upsurge in small firms, where entering new markets is the norm. Unfortunately, growth runs counter to the anemic state of global economic improvement.

Networks offer two striking ways out of the world's predicament. Short-term growth can increase through cross-boundary ties—joint ventures, strategic alliances, virtual corporations, flexible business networks. Alliances expand capabilities and opportunities while limiting risk. You can try things without putting your whole business at stake. "Small giants," groups of small companies that work together to do what they can't do alone, have learned very well how to limit risk in this way.

Longer term, networking generates new wealth based on social capital, the interpersonal good will and trust that grease cooperation. The more business relationships exist among companies, the faster social capital accumulates.

- *Creating breakthrough products, entering new markets, and achieving high-performance operations will be tougher than ever.*

To achieve real growth, companies will have to think differently about every aspect of their businesses. Breakthroughs, whether in products or in markets, will require genuine creativity. Persistent, interdisciplinary hard work, not dumb luck, will prevail. The norm for developing new business strategies will be to rethink, revisit, and refine purpose. Individuals, teams, and business units of all sizes will need both committed independence and a challenging but risk-supporting environment that fosters co-opetition—the conjunction of competition and cooperation, creativity, and getting an idea to market.

> • *As organizations reach optimal size, they will seek qualitative development rather than quantitative growth.*

Growth in numbers is great when you're small and the limits are beyond view. All growth is not great if you are already big. Contrary to 1980s' propaganda, no one can repeal the "limits to growth" on earth. Population continues its steep ascent in the predominantly southern Third World, while consumerism continues to mount in the predominantly northern developed world.[8]

Buckminster Fuller's dictum, "Do more with less," proves ever more true. Social capital will drive growth by "funding" new wealth through creativity and innovation. Intelligence, flexibility, diversification, and aspirations for a higher quality of life are survival skills in markets with limited physical growth.

> • *Organizations will regard purpose as their richest natural resource. They will mine it with new tools, techniques, methods, and models.*

Explicit purpose is the new source of legitimacy, replacing the brute force of hierarchy and the rules and regulations of bureaucracy. A whole new advice industry has sprung up for vision, strategy, and work process design to make purpose explicit. New tools—technical and conceptual, high tech and low, personal and public—will help people make their purpose more explicit. Shelves will be clogged with how-to books and products on mining and refining the raw resources of commitment and cooperation.[9]

In time, of course, these techniques will become the "Old Way" and barriers for the later 21st century to overcome. Meanwhile, we need to wean ourselves from bureaucratic policies and hierarchical commands.

Members Need a New Look

The 21st-century organization holds people and organizations in high esteem while enhancing their *self*-esteem, independent and interdependent, the second of the five teamnet principles.

> • *Team implementations will continue to fail at alarming rates.*

For the downsized organization a team structure is no longer an option; it is a necessity. The downsizing trend that began in the late 1980s is different from previous cycles of job contraction. Not only have specific-skill jobs disappeared for good, but a whole layer of jobs—middle management—is a fraction of its former size. Once you have laid an organization flat, eliminating most of middle management, you can't go back. Unlike other change initiatives that have failed, delayering leaves organizations without a fallback position. They simply cannot return to the organization they dismantled. So, teams scramble to fill in the gap—exhausted, overworked, unprepared, and lacking an overall architecture.

Where there is more than one team, there is a teamnet, whether it is recognized as such or not. Thus, the failure of any part of a teamnet can be traced to one or more of the Five Teamnet Principles. Purpose may be unclear. Members may be too dependent. Communication may be inadequate. There may be too few leaders. The team may have tried to operate at only one level. More broadly, teams in organizations that deplete social capital also will fail. Successful teams thrive in a rich social life, where associations are plentiful.

> • *Companies will need to reinstill loyalty and motivate their people anew to do extremely innovative work.*

Loyalty is at an all-time low in many firms due to short-term employment and career uncertainty. Few organizations have found effective ways to remedy this situation. Downsizing takes a toll in fear far wider than the immediate impact on those laid off.

Teams—and networks of teams—offer smaller-scale arenas in which to build trust and clarify purpose. An enterprisewide plan for converting to a more team-network organization itself gives hope. It offers a vision of a future better than that of hierarchy-bureaucracy. Without the promise of change, all the survivors of downsizing see is more work for fewer people.

> • *Individuals will rebel against the unending, ever-increasing demand for higher levels of performance.*

High performance all the time is the fantasy of Supermen and Superwomen everywhere. Great ideal, completely impractical. People and organizations that run wide awake at top speed all the time do not survive for long. Burnout afflicts individuals and groups alike. Life has rhythms that can be stretched but not ignored.

High-performance, intensive interaction also isolates teams from the rest of the world. Peak periods of performance strain great ecologies of nonteam relationships that are put on hold, missed, broken, and otherwise depleted. To compensate, people will acknowledge this conflict and begin to address it. Rest will become a legitimate activity, both for individuals and for groups.

> • *Independence will spread as cooperation increases.*

Globally, East and West are polar tendencies in regard to the individual and group, the fundamental social dynamic. The East puts the needs of society ahead of those of the individual, while the West emphasizes the rights of the individual. Networking embraces both. In theory and practice, it integrates these polarities. "Me" and "we" are equally important. Individual and group together process the fundamental dynamic of organizations.

A dramatic, large-scale example of independence with cooperation warranted this front-page headline in *The Wall Street Journal*: "Global Paradox; Growth of Trade Binds Nations, but It Also Can Spur Separatism; A World of 500 Countries?"[10] From Catalonians in Spain to Quebeçois in Canada to Wallonians in Belgium to Tamils in Sri Lanka, "It's a paradox of global proportions," the article began, "the closer that trade and technology bind nations together, the bolder the moves to break nations apart."

GETTING LINKS IN SYNCH

The third teamnet principle, with its counsel to "just add links," influences both people and technology.

• *Physical links will continue to explode—from one to one to many to many—into digital convergence in the year 2001.*

"Digital convergence" is a bundle of ideas linked by the recognition that all information can be rendered in "digital" (also called "computer," "electronic," or "binary") form for storing, processing, and transmitting. "Anything, anytime, anywhere" is how Bill Johnson, now IBM's networking hardware manager, put it in 1987 when he led Digital Equipment Corporation's networking effort as vice president.[11] Electronic "pipes" of awesome capacity to the home, satellites connecting remote villages, the total mobility of all communication, all coming soon.

Digital convergence is one of the great breaking business stories of the 1990s. We are witnessing a global formation of *digital keiretsu*, an amalgamation like the Japanese model where large numbers of firms work together in vertical alliances. Clusters of alliances swarm around core giants like Time-Warner, Viacom, and TCI in cable and entertainment, AT&T and the Baby Bells, game players like Sony and Nintendo, richly connected computer companies like IBM and Apple, and central casting media mavens like Paramount and Disney. From book publishers to software to chip makers, from newspapers to TV to toys, from mobile to movies to online services and the Information Superhighway—it's all part of the rich interactive brew out of which digital teamnets are being created on a grand scale.

- *Companies will have to learn how to share important information with all employees.*

"In a command and control organization," says Levi Strauss's CEO, Robert Haas, "people protect knowledge because it's their claim to distinction. But we share as much information as we possibly can throughout the company."[12]

"Only the information necessary to do your job" means something very different in a secretive society than it does in a culture of openness and availability to the point of overload. Cross-boundary responsibilities, the need to understand the Big Picture, and the need to adopt the CEO view lead more people to have access to more information, a philosophy that has led Levi Strauss to five straight years of record profits.

Without information, people won't be able to do their jobs, take responsible actions, or make choices to benefit the larger organization. Synergy, serendipity, and creativity can come from anywhere. One reflection of this trend is "open book management." Here all the people in an organization know how they fit into the bottom line.

> • *Just catching up to the learning organization?*
> *Rev it up; we'll be moving on to the "fast*
> *learning" organization.*

Speed is of the essence—more so than ever. Wider appreciation of "knowledge work" lifts the bar. To keep ahead, organizations consciously strive to become smarter.

Learning alone will not be adequate unless organizations can rapidly assimilate and commercialize information. More information will come from more sources. Most of it will come from across boundaries of various sorts as "not invented here" will become the norm. More people will have access to the same information sooner, so the ability to use it rapidly for business advantage will provide the competitive edge. Learn, apply; learn, apply.

> • *The backlash will mushroom against purely*
> *high-tech approaches to resolving problems*
> *and meeting challenges.*

Installing a computer network or voice mail system does not guarantee that suddenly everyone will start working together. We first heard the early warnings of this rumble inside Digital Equipment Corporation in 1988. A report from one of their largest accounts held a startling discovery. The customer had studied productivity gains from their $2 billion information technology investment and found, strikingly, none. Further, they found the source of the problem to be not in the technology but rather in having ignored people and the organization of work.

Today fewer believe that technology alone can solve people problems.[13] Networks provide a common language to approach organizational and technology issues—that is, "high-touch" and "high-tech" together.[14] "Business spent $1 trillion on information technology in the last decade—but showed little gain in efficiency. Now, productivity is finally bursting out, thanks to better software and a reorganization of work itself," says *Business Week*.[15]

- *Social capital will be seen as a new source of wealth. This recognition will develop slowly, then suddenly catch on as success stories accumulate, reaching critical mass at the century's turn.*

Tom Melohn, "head sweeper" at North American Tool and Die, who forged *The New Partnership*,[16] is a harbinger of a new way to build companies. Melohn based his company's turnaround of a traditional machine shop simply and practically on applied honesty and trust, for himself and for his associates, vendors, and customers. A culture where "we're all bosses" requires four "currencies," he says: "equality, mutual respect, dignity, and self-worth."

Social capital says that history is important, but it is not the only factor shaping the future. History is where you start, but there are many ways to accumulate trust and develop relationships. As more organizations, regions, and other islands of trust achieve high performance, a high quality of life, and visibility, social capital finally will burst into public consciousness.

LEADING TRENDS

The fourth principle, multiple leadership, challenges people's ability to cooperate, requiring them to behave with maturity, a hallmark of people in 21st-century organizations. "In a heterogeneous group, maturity is essential," writes Marc Hequet in *Training*.[17]

• *A new style of leadership is emerging. The
old-fashioned just-do-as-I-say hierarchy
doesn't work across company lines.
Meanwhile, those to be led are of a
completely new ilk.*

"The New Post-Heroic Leadership: Pull yourself off the pedestal
and share the power at last," reads the cover of *Fortune*.[18] Inside, Tom
Peters says, "People realize now that they really must do it to survive."
Warren Bennis agrees: "Leaders must learn to change the nature of
power and how it's employed." Like the Information Age, the new
leadership has moved from Sunday supplement articles about the
future to today's reality and basis for survivability.

W.L. Gore & Associates is a prime example of a successful organization that started with a dramatically different postindustrial approach to leadership. Everyone who works there is an "associate,"
and everyone has a sponsor.[19] Other examples, like Southwest Air-
lines, the young company that transformed itself during rapid growth,
and Levi Strauss, a classic industrial icon that overcame all the constraints of a traditional enterprise, indicate that any firm can reinvent
leadership.

• *A new generation of leaders is being
groomed. They come from a much more
diverse pool, bringing vast cultural differences
with them.*

Biodiversity has a social counterpart in cultural diversity: The number of sovereign countries has nearly doubled in half a decade. Children in the Los Angeles school system speak more than 100 languages.
There are more than 20,000 separate Christian denominations. Asian
decision making differs from African; Scandinavian business meetings

are unlike those in Brazil. Highly collective societies, like Japan and Singapore, must trade with highly individualistic ones, like the United States and France. Russia rumbles relentlessly as its eastern neighbor, China, where one-fifth of the world's population resides, still clings to the 19th-century industrial invention of communism and the awesome bureaucracy that it spawned.

And even now, we haven't called out the force of women. Still locked out of the executive suite and the boardroom, women nonetheless dominate the new work force. Women manage differently from men. They balance different priorities, converse differently, reach conclusions through different routes, and, some scientists believe, even have different cognitive processes.

Organizations without diversity at the top will fail in the 21st century.

> • *New jobs and leadership roles are being invented to manage the burgeoning, bewildering webs of connections and relationships.*

Coordinators, brokers, liaisons, facilitators, consultants, catalysts, linkers, matchmakers, and "netweavers"[20] all represent new types of jobs. Colin Hastings, a London-based consultant who has looked extensively at new networking roles, has identified these in addition: mentors, integrators, *animateurs* (similar to what Apple Computer once called "evangelists"), counterparts (liaisons), developers, investigators, and disseminators.[21]

The explosive expansion of connections breeds new types of jobs. But the jobs will not come easily. People don't want to pay for networking, which is all too often regarded as a "free" activity, not requiring compensation to remain economically viable. But "networking is not for free," as Ulf Fagerquist, a nuclear physicist and systems designer, told us long ago. Creative funding of these new positions will firmly establish this trend.

> • *The top will be the last to truly team. Some*
> *executives will continue to be embarrassments*
> *to their corporate change*
> *efforts.*

"The true team at the top is still hard to find," says Deborah Ancona, associate professor of organizational studies at MIT.[22] It's no wonder. Executives occupy the last bastion of vertical control. They are the designated officers in the owner's army. Inescapably, they constitute the irreducible hierarchy in the organization. Executive teams always must vigorously manage the "both/and"—*both* executing hierarchical responsibilities whenever necessary *and* showing team leadership whenever possible.

LEAPING LEVELS

The fifth principle, integrating levels, is both the most conceptual and the most practical. Organizations will not survive in the Age of the Network without using it.

> • *Layer cutting just for the sake of cost cutting*
> *will destroy organizations. Team-networks*
> *work best across multiple levels.*

Don't get us wrong: relative to traditional steep hierarchy-bureaucracies, hierarchies in teamnets are much flatter. But in networks, each level of the organization requires its own integrity and source of self-reliance. Members at each level have a characteristic independence and range of purposeful decision making.

One company that embodies the careful use of levels is Asea Brown Boveri. With a quarter of a million employees in over 140 countries,

ABB has just five levels of organization: teams, profit centers, companies, countries/business areas (which house its matrix), and an executive committee.[23] Each level has its own economics and management integrity from a business point of view, with its appropriate purposes, loyalties, and scales of operation.

• *Single-solution approaches to management are out; more holistic, integrated views are in.*

Complexity makes a mockery of "magic bullets," "quick fixes," and "one size fits all" solutions. As complexity becomes more manifest, people are adapting creatively. They adopt strategies that lead to greater awareness of how all the elements of their businesses interrelate.

Everyone in the enterprise needs to be aware of the whole, not just the few at the top. Even key customers, suppliers, and other significant external partners need companywide knowledge to be effective contributors. At the same time, companies need more creative models to protect the privacy required for competitiveness.

ON HOLONOMY

Bill Miller has seven desks at home. The director of research and business development at Steelcase, Inc., the Grand Rapids, Michigan, office furniture company, Miller has visions of "body-mounted" computing. He asks questions like "How do you network a billion things together?"

"I'm one of the guys who created local area networks like Ethernet," Miller says to explain himself. Now he is thinking about how to help people work more effectively. So, he troubles over networks that are both self-configuring and self-diagnosing, about such topics as "ubiquitous" computing, which means being able to be online anytime, anywhere. He predicts that before long, our desks will contain 10,000 electronic devices—at the microprocessor level. This may not be what you expect to hear from a company like Steelcase, the first to manufacture filing cabinets on a grand scale. Look at the company's mission statement today, whose goal is: "to help people work more effectively."

"We believe that there's a major transformation in business management," Miller says, "and it's all based on holons."

Miller works at the juncture of the physical, social, and information environments that people and groups inhabit. For Miller, the holon crosses conceptual boundaries of these different disciplines; it shows up quite concretely in the design of their office products.

At Steelcase, R&D represents another trend, that of *intellectual* development.

* *Networking will accelerate the resurgence of interest in systems theory—both for its human touch and for its scientific approach to management.*

"Holons" Are Wholes and Parts

Everything is naturally a holon, which means "whole-part," hol-on. A holon is a whole that is also a part—like a person, an individual whole yet a social part; like a cell or an atom.

A company is a whole but is part of an industry. A department is a whole of groups, yet also part of a larger organization. A state is a federal part and a whole made up of localities. Families are parts of communities and wholes of parents and children.

Only at the extremes of quantum physics and cosmology are there (maybe) *smallest* parts/relationships and *largest* wholes/patterns; everything else is a holon.

The word "holon" was coined by Arthur Koestler, the giant intellect, artist, and scientist,[24] who wanted a small word to express a very big and somewhat awkward idea implicit in the nature of everything: systems within systems within systems. Herbert Simon called this principle the "architecture of complexity" (see chapter 3). For the architect Christopher Alexander, it is the foundation of "a pattern language" for design.[25] For Steelcase, it means designing modules within components within systems for people within groups within organizations.

Systems theory works across boundaries. It captures insights, principles, and laws that span both traditional sciences, such as physics and biology, and newer sciences, such as information theory and cognition.

But it's hard to make the word "system" very popular. For good reason, people hate "the system." It does nothing but aggravate them. Just think about going to renew your driver's license, or trying to get a bill corrected, or, heaven forbid, having to engage with the legal system. Systems, in their common connotation, deserve their stereotypes as vast, impersonal, impenetrable, and too often inhumane. Indeed, people often confuse organizational systems generally with the apparatus of the traditional hierarchy-bureaucracy.

Networks are systems by another name.[26] They have the same cross-boundary, cross-science characteristics as systems. Instead of being "black boxes" with opaque boundaries, networks are "glass boxes" with translucent and transparent perimeters. The innards of networks are immediately evident and accessible to observers; they offer another language for very open systems.

Nearly a century after the revolution in the natural sciences begun by physics, the human sciences still are in desperate need of a robust conceptual foundation. The incredibly obsolete Newtonian framework is still rampant in human affairs. Systems theory, network style, offers a direct link to modern thinking in the natural sciences. Its conceptual architecture and practice incorporate the complexity and ambiguity required in the human sciences.

Systems theory is cross-disciplinary in the extreme.[27] There are now many general systems theories, each developed to explain large chunks of everything. In *Holonomy: A Human Systems Theory*,[28] Jeff compares many of the prevailing systems theories in the search of their common patterns.

Many theorists—including great first-generation systems thinkers such as Bateson, Bohm, Boulding, Fraser, Forrester, Koestler, Laszlo, Miller, Polyani, Prigogine, Rapoport, Simon, von Bertalanffy, and Whyte—recognize one or both of two fundamental patterns in systems:

Levels and complements: Where there are system structures, *there are hierarchies of levels. Where there are system* processes, *there are complementary relationships.*

An organization as a structure has levels, from the entry one to the CEO, and is enmeshed in many more, larger levels. Whether small groups, hierarchies, bureaucracies, or networks, human organizations of all sorts are *holon*-archical. People and companies alike are holons, both wholes and parts.

An organization is also a system of processes. In business, we act in complementary relationships all the time: buyer and seller, customer and supplier, the law of supply and demand. These counterbalances underlie basic business processes and drive markets. Balancing (stabilizing) and reinforcing (amplifying) feedback loops are the stuff of systems dynamics.[29]

The ancient yin–yang symbol, which we adapt here to make the point, shows how we can compete and cooperate at the same time using the Five Teamnet Principles. As independent people, we compete; as a group striving toward shared purpose, we communicate and cooperate. By connecting the black and white centers, which traditionally remain separate, competition and cooperation become co-opetition, a holon in action, a dynamic expression of these concepts. The whole–part is fundamental to networking.

> *Structure and process also are complements,
> snapshots of persistence over time. Networks
> are the structure and networking is the process,
> sometimes particlelike and sometimes wavelike.*

Our favorite example of levels and complements is, naturally, our own: independent and complementary as woman and man, we are a couple, another level. Our marriage perseveres through the chaos of our lives, our own "process." In time, as a couple, we give birth to our daughters, Miranda and Eliza, another level (and in that order). With them, we form a new whole as a family, with additional dynamics of parents and children.

The dynamics of the person and the group churn in all human processes. "If you rethought the office from the ground up, and said that the team is the primary contributor, you would think of the office very differently," said Mike Brill, president of a Buffalo, New York, think tank on office work and office design.[30]

Like many other intelligent organizations, Steelcase demonstrates

CO-OPETITION AS A COMPLEMENT

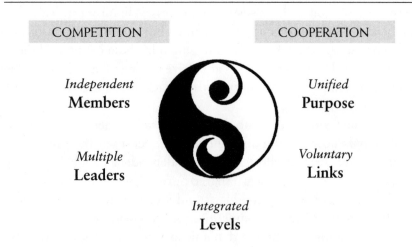

COMPETITION   COOPERATION

Independent   *Unified*
Members   **Purpose**

Multiple   *Voluntary*
Leaders   **Links**

Integrated
Levels

this profound understanding of both human and technology systems. Steelcase is stepping out of the Industrial Era, with its rigid caricature of a standardized person at a standardized desk, and into the Knowledge Era, where people work both independently and in groups, here and there, at a desk, on the phone, and with a computer, standing, sitting, and even pacing.

Steelcase's highly flexible teamnet furniture system puts an organization on wheels, meaning that each module—from the chairs to the white boards to the individual offices—is completely movable and reconfigurable. Private spaces, which they call "personal harbor," combine with public spaces, which they call "commons," for ongoing teamwork.[31]

In bureaucracy, public and private are separate. In networks, they are complements.

PERSONAL HARBOR™ AND TEAM COMMONS

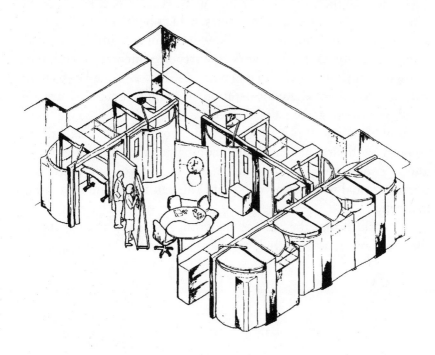

SOUL SEARCH

One thought has tugged on us from the day we consciously began working on networks in 1979: values. What values motivate these new organizations? Unifying purpose is a focused, specific way of talking about values, which are diffuse and general. Values are very big and pervasive, and they give rise to the last trend.

• *The search for soul will accelerate and move from the individual and family to organizations of all sorts and sizes.*

People seek meaning in their life. Work is a big part of life, sometimes most of it. The search for values, held at bureaucratic bay by the strict separation of home and work, will continue to invade organizations. In the Age of the Network, the trend to integration with independence inevitably will lead to a more holistic view of all parts of life working together. The consideration of "family issues" is just one small part of integrating life and work.

"Soul" is a place holder for what Christopher Alexander calls the "quality without a name."[32] Vital companies with a culture of trust and openness have it. You can't name it, but you know a strong organizational soul when you see it. You can feel it and sense it; it's magnetic.

Networks bridge the self and the group, the daily and the eternal, the mundane and the sacred, and carry us into the 21st century.

NOTES

Chapter 1

1. The quote on how technology drives organizational change is from technology expert Kathleen Barry Albertini's manuscript notes, April 27, 1994.
2. We thank Edmond Molloy, a Dublin, Ireland, organizational consultant, for sending us this supplement to the *Irish Times*. See "Networks of Power," December 29, 1993, p. 7.
3. The quote on corporate espionage is from "Global Spy Networks Eavesdrop on Projects of Petroleum Firms," by William M. Carley, *The Wall Street Journal*, January 6, 1994, p. A1.
4. The quote on multiple leadership roles is from "Could AT&T Rule the World?" by David Kirkpatrick, *Fortune*, May 17, 1993, p. 57.
5. Eastman Chemical Company's organizational chart is shown in detail in chapter 3, p. 75.
6. The quote from Eastman's Chairman and CEO, Earnest Deavenport, is from "The Horizontal Corporation," by John A. Byrne, *Business Week*, December 20, 1993, p. 80.
7. For a fast paced, "multimedia"-style look at the new organization, see *The Tom Peters Seminar: Crazy Times Call for Crazy Organizations*, by Tom Peters (New York: Vintage Books, 1994), p. 5.
8. For a review of research collaborations, see "What's the Word in the Lab? Collaborate," by Peter Coy et al., *Business Week*, June 27, 1994, p. 79.
9. All quotes about the lab without walls are from Frank Starmer's December 30, 1993, e-mail message.
10. For an excellent source on building networking relationships, see *Networking Smart: How to Build Relationships for Personal and Organizational Success*, by Wayne E. Baker (New York: McGraw-Hill, 1994).
11. For more on the issues of leadership and coordination in networks, see *The Challenge of the Resource Exchange Network: From Concept to Action*, by Seymour B. Sarason and Elizabeth Lorentz (San Francisco: Jossey-Bass, 1979), chapter 5.

12. The quote on why medieval networks came together is from *Making Democracy Work: Civic Traditions in Modern Italy*, by Robert D. Putnam, p. 126, quoted from Daniel Waley, *The Italian City-Republics* (New York: Longman, 1978), pp. 97, 114.

13. For an extensive treatment of the global flexible business network movement, see our third book, *The TeamNet Factor: Bringing the Power of Boundary Crossing Into the Heart of Your Business* (Essex Junction, VT: Oliver Wight, 1993), chapter 7.

14. For more information on how to eliminate waste in organizations, see *The Profit Potential: Taking High Performance to the Bottom Line*, by Carol J. McNair (Essex Junction, VT: Oliver Wight/Omneo, 1994).

15. The identification of unnecessary overhead created by checkers is from Marion Metcalf's "Comments on [*Age of the Network*] Manuscript," June 16, 1994.

16. Dr. Günther Singer is an organizational consultant with Networking Design Institute, Feldhofgasse 28, A-9020 Klagenfurt, Austria. Telephone: 43-463-37730; fax: 43-463-319450; e-mail: gsinger@ndi.co.at.

17. For an excellent discussion of networks, see Virginia H. Hine's seminal paper, "The Basic Paradigm of a Future Socio-Cultural System," *World Issues*, Spring, 1977 (Center for the Study of Democratic Institutions, Santa Barbara, CA). See also *People, Power, Change: Movements of Social Transformation*, by Luther P. Gerlach and Virginia H. Hine (New York: Bobbs-Merrill, 1970).

Chapter 2

1. The quote on the decline in the national fire rate is from "Firefighters' mission a burning issue," by Chris Black, *The Boston Globe*, December 11, 1994, p. 9.

2. Statistics on the Internet are from "Fun facts and figures from the Internet Index," compiled by Win Treese, "The Voxbox," *The Boston Globe*, December 30, 1993, p. 50.

3. For more on the international Mars project, see "US Joins with 3 Other Nations to Work Together on Plans for Mars Missions," by David L. Chandler, *The Boston Globe*, May 31, 1993, p. 28.

4. In 1994, *The Economist* carried an eye-catching ad for Airbus, which included an artist's rendition of the four countries involved in the venture.

5. For more detail on AT&T's operations, see "Could AT&T Rule the World?" by David Kirkpatrick, *Fortune*, May 17, 1993, p. 62.

6. The quote on the relationship between the Information Age and culture is from "Bell Atlantic's Virtual Work Force," by Raymond W. Smith, *The Futurist*, March–April, 1994, p. 13.

7. For more on the relationship between proximity and collaboration, see *Managing the Flow of Technology: Technology Transfer and the Dissemination of Technological Information within the R&D Organization*, by Thomas J. Allen (Cambridge, MA: MIT Press, 1977).

8. Further work on proximity and the probability of collaboration has been conducted by researchers at Bell Communications and the University of Arizona, who built on Allen's study. See "Patterns of Contact and Communication in Scientific Research Collaboration," by Robert Kraut and Carmen Egido, Bell Communications Research, Inc., and Jolene Galegher, University of Arizona, *Computer Supported Cooperative Work*, Conference Proceedings, (New York: Association for Computing Machinery, 1988).

Chapter 3

1. Responsible Care[sm] is a registered service mark of the Chemical Manufacturers Association.

2. Information on Eastman's network of interlocking teams was drawn from Eastman Chemical Company's Malcolm Baldrige National Quality Award information sheet, "1993 Award Winner," provided by Robert C. Joines, vice president, quality, 1993.

3. Detailed numbers on Eastman's supplier teams are from Joines's manuscript notes, April 4, 1994.

4. Herbert Simon, one of the great intellectual pioneers of the Information Age (and 1978 recipient of the Nobel Prize for economics), wrote the parable to explain why the evolution of complexity so often takes on the sets-within-sets form. In "The Architecture of Complexity" (Yearbook of the Society for General Systems Research, 1965, reprinted from the Proceedings of the American Philosophical Society, 1962), Simon explains "hierarchy" as a mathematical generalization about levels of a system independent of any level itself.

5. The "Taylored" pun alludes to Frederick Winslow Taylor, founder of "scientific" management based on reductionist principles.

6. For more information on Eastman's quality effort, see *Eastman Chemical Company Application Summary*, 1993 Malcolm Baldrige National

Quality Award (Kingsport, TN: Eastman Chemical Company, Publication ECC-68, January, 1994), p. 2.

Chapter 4

1. The quote on functions disappearing at EBC Industries is from a June 2, 1994, note written by Harry Brown.
2. For more on "The Nine Principles of War," see *Operations*, 14 June 1993, AR FM 100-5 (Army Operations Manual).
3. The description of VISA comes from remarks by Dee Hock, president and CEO emeritus, VISA International, at a meeting convened by the Joyce Foundation, October 11, 1993. We thank Joel Getzendanner, formerly of the Joyce Foundation, and Rebecca Adamson, founder of First Nations Financial Project, for introducing us to Hock's work.
4. The quote on networks connecting people is from a Cayman Systems advertisement that appeared in *MacWeek*, on February 21, 1994.
5. The quote on "ever-shifting" teams is from "Bell Atlantic's Virtual Work Force," by Raymond W. Smith, *The Futurist*, March–April 1994, p. 13.
6. The quote on networking as a key competitive strategy is from Safeguard Scientifics, Inc.'s, 1988 Annual Report.
7. Many other examples of both large and small companies are described in *The TeamNet Factor*, some in considerable detail, especially in chapters 2 through 7. The chart that appears here is parallel to the chart in *The TeamNet Factor*, p. 309, redone here with new examples.
8. For more on optimum size, see *Rebirth of the Corporation*, by D. Quinn Mills (New York: Wiley, 1991), pp. 3, 8, 30.
9. For more on "continuous improvement involving everyone," see *Kaizen: The Keys to Japan's Competitive Success*, by Masaaki Imai (New York: McGraw-Hill, 1986).
10. For an extensive discussion of the topic, see *The End of Bureaucracy and the Rise of the Intelligent Organization*, by Gifford and Elizabeth Pinchot (San Francisco: Berrett-Koehler, 1993), p. 175.
11. The quote on the intelligence of markets is from "Let's Turn Organizations into Markets!" by William E. Halal, *The Futurist*, May–June, 1994, p. 9.
12. For more on virtual corporations, see *The Virtual Corporation: Structuring and Revitalizing the Corporation for the 21st Century*, by William H. Davidow and Michael S. Malone (New York: HarperCollins, 1992).

13. For a description of life at Chiat/Day, see "The Virtual Agency," by Charles Rubin, *MacWeek*, December 13, 1993, p. 22.
14. The quote on Chrysler as a virtual enterprise is from "Chrysler's Man of Many Parts Cuts Costs," by Douglas Lavin, *The Wall Street Journal*, May 17, 1993, p. B1.
15. For more on Intel's alliances, see "The Coming Clash of Logic," *The Economist*, July 3, 1993, p. 23.
16. For much more on flexible business networks, see *The TeamNet Factor*, chapters 6 and 7.
17. For more on Toshiba's alliances, see "How Toshiba Makes Alliances Work," by Brent Schendler, *Fortune*, October 4, 1993, pp. 116–122.

Chapter 5

1. The complete quote, one of Dwight D. Eisenhower's favorite maxims, is "In preparing for battle I have always found that plans are useless, but planning is indispensable." *The Columbia Dictionary of Quotations* (New York: Columbia University Press, 1993), p. 688.
2. David Kearns, former CEO of Xerox, appeared in *Challenge to America,* a four-part TV series produced and moderated by Hedrick Smith, aired on PBS in January, 1994.
3. See chapters 8–10 of *The Teamnet Factor* for more on the development process, the startup phase, and a detailed launch methodology with associated planning tools.
4. For more on the need for transitional times in the workplace, see *Making the Most of Change*, by William Bridges (Reading, MA: Addison-Wesley, 1991). Our thanks to Sue Goran for referring us to this work.

Chapter 6

1. This quote, "information wants to be free," is from a speech by Stewart Brand, publisher of *The Whole Earth Catalog* and founder of The Well, the computer conferencing system based in Sausalito, California, given at the Western Behavioral Sciences Institute, La Jolla, California, July, 1984.
2. The "reinventing government" report is available in bookstores and directly from the U.S. government, in both hard copy and electronic form. To order the hard copy version, *Creating a Government That Works Better & Costs Less: From Red Tape to Results*, Report of the National Per-

formance Review, contact the U.S. Government Printing Office, Superintendent of Documents, Mail Stop: SSOP, Washington, DC 20402-9328. For the electronic version, use the Internet: type "gopher ace.esusda.gov" and then choose "Americans Communicating Electronically," followed by "National Performance Review Information."

3. See *Reinventing Government: How the Entrepreneurial Spirit Is Transforming the Public Sector* by David Osborne and Ted Gaebler (New York: Plume/Penguin, 1993). Osborne served as a key contributor to the National Performance Review.

4. The quote "We can't solve 21st-century problems with 19th-century organizations" is inspired by this quote from Albert Einstein: "The significant problems we face cannot be solved at the same level of thinking we were at when we created them."

5. The U.S. Treasury Department's Mike Serlin, assistant commissioner, financial management service, first proposed the name "NetResults" to the 40 people gathered for the third day of the launch. "When I said it, the group applauded, and that was that!" he explained. Serlin also describes being in a network as analogous to performing in repertory theater, where people are adept at playing many roles.

6. Vice President Gore's support of NetResults has been communicated to National Performance Review staff members in various meetings.

7. To obtain a list of National Performance Review materials, send a one-line e-mail message via the Internet to "almanac@esusda.gov" with the following text: "send npr catalog" or send a letter via U.S. mail to National Performance Review, 750 17th Street, NW, Washington, DC 20006; telephone: 202-632-0150.

8. In addition to the contacts listed in note 2, NetResults information is available on MetaNet (telephone: 703-243-6622); CAPACCESS, an electronic service provided by George Washington University (telephone: 202-986-2065); and FedWorld, a U.S. Department of Commerce service (telephone: 703-487-4608).

9. Robert Maslyn gave this description of the "resident solo expert" in the U.S. federal bureaucracy at TeamNet Workshop No. 3, April 7, 1994, Cambridge, Massachusetts.

10. For a further discussion of holons, see "On Holonomy," chapter 9, this book, p. 226.

11. For an excellent treatment of the relationship of quantum physics and chaos to organizations, see *Leadership and the New Science: Learning*

about Organization from an Orderly Universe, by Margaret J. Wheatley (San Francisco: Berrett-Koehler, 1992).

12. The phrase "hinge of history" was first used by biophysicist John Rader Platt in his book *The Step to Man* (New York: Wiley, 1966). Platt was one of the earliest to project the spread of HIV along this same trajectory.

13. We thank O. W. Markley, Ph.D., P.E., professor, Futures Research, University of Houston, Clear Lake, 2700 Bay Area Boulevard, Houston, TX, 77058, for the "Hinge of History" chart.

14. For the original work on "limits to growth," see the ground-breaking Club of Rome study, *Limits to Growth*, by Donella H. Meadows, Dennis L. Meadows, Jørgen Randers, and William W. Behrens III (New York: New American Library, 1972).

15. Among the seminal works on how organizations evolve in relationship to the environment is F. E. Emery and E.C. Trist's article, "The Causal Texture of Organizational Environment," *Human Relations*, Vol. 18, August, 1965, pp. 20–26.

16. An even earlier classic study of change and organizational structure is *The Management of Innovation* by, Tom Burns and G. M. Stalker. (London: Tavistock, 1961). See also *Organization and Environment*, by Paul R. Lawrence and Jay W. Lorsch (Boston: Division of Research, Graduate School of Business Administration, Harvard University, 1967) for observations on the relationship of internal structure to uncertainty.

17. Our chart "Environmental Pace of Change Assessment" combines and adapts Emery and Trist's and Burns and Stalker's classic research instruments (see notes 15 and 16).

18. The quote on doing business with AT&T is from "Could AT&T Rule the World?" by David Kirkpatrick, *Fortune*, May 17, 1993, p. 55.

Chapter 7

1. The "only connect" quote is from *Howards End*, by E. M. Forster (London: Edward Arnold, 1910).

2. The quote on "creative juices" flowing is from Frank Starmer's December 30, 1994, e-mail message.

3. We use the words "virus" and "worm" interchangeably.

4. "Specifically, [the worm] invaded Sun 3 and VAX computers running versions of the Berkeley 4.3 UNIX operating system containing the TCP/

IP Internet protocols. Its sole purpose was to enter new machines by bypassing authentication procedures and to propagate new copies of itself. It was prolific, generating on the order of hundreds of thousands of copies among several thousand machines worldwide. It did not destroy information, give away passwords, or implant Trojan horses for later damage," wrote Peter J. Denning in "The Internet Worm," *American Scientist*, March–April, 1989, pp. 126–128.

5. The worm gained unwelcome entry into machines via a Unix protocol known as "fingerd," which keeps the directory of all the people on a particular system.

6. For a spellbinding account of how the worm was stopped, see "With Microscope and Tweezers: The Worm from MIT's Perspective," by Jon Rochlis and Mark Eichin, *Communications of the ACM* [Association for Computing Machinery], Vol. 32, No. 6, June, 1989, pp. 689–698.

7. Rochlis and Mark Eichin also do an excellent job of evaluating what was learned from the worm.

8. Norris Parker Smith's description of the Internet as "anarchy that works" is from his article "Jockeying for Position on the Data Highway," *Upside*, May, 1993, p. 51.

9. As of July, 1994, *Dateline*'s e-mail address is "dateline@news.nbc.com."

10. The description of Doug Lea's home–office is from his e-mail message of March 31, 1994.

11. For more on Christopher Alexander's extraordinary work, see his two seminal books, *A Pattern Language* (New York: Oxford University Press, 1977) and *The Timeless Way of Building* (New York: Oxford University Press, 1979). We thank Doug Lea and Lyn Montague for pointing us to Alexander's work.

12. The e-mail address for *Utne Reader* is "salons@utnereader.com."

13. For an excellent description of life on the Internet, see *The Virtual Community: Homesteading on the Electronic Frontier*, by Howard Rheingold (Reading, MA: Addison-Wesley, 1993). Rheingold's Internet address is "hlr@well.sf.ca.us."

14. MetaSystems Design Group, which runs MetaNet, can be reached at 2000 North 15th Street, Suite 103, Arlington, VA 22201; telephone: 703-243-6622. Lisa Kimball's Internet address is "lisa@tmn.com."

15. All quotes from Lisa Kimball are from her April 22, 1994, e-mail message.

16. The Kaypro belonged to the Washington, D.C.-based former Episcopal priest Harrison Owen, an organizational consultant and developer of "Open Space" conferences.

17. For an extensive treatment of social network analysis, see *Social Structure and Network Analysis*, edited by Peter V. Marsden and Nan Lin (Beverly Hills, CA: Sage, 1982), p. 9.

18. Among the tools for analyzing networks are those explained in *Applied Network Analysis: A Methodological Introduction*, by Ronald S. Burt and Michael J. Minor and Associates (Beverly Hills, CA: Sage, 1983). The interdisciplinary International Network for Social Network Analysis represents many of the currents in this broad trend.

19. For a discussion of networks as an antidote to loneliness, see *Extending Families: The Social Networks of Parents and Their Children*, by Moncrieff M. Cochran et al. (Cambridge, England: Cambridge University Press, 1990). We are grateful to Elizabeth Lorentz for pointing us to Cochran's work, which shows that denser webs of connections make people happier.

20. For an in-depth treatment of the coordinator role, see *The Challenge of the Resource Exchange Network*, by Seymour Sarason and Elizabeth Lorentz (San Francisco: Jossey-Bass, 1979; Cambridge, MA: Brookline Books, 1988), p. 146.

21. In *The Creation of Settings and the Future Societies* (San Francisco: Jossey-Bass, 1972), Sarason defines "a setting as when two or more people get together in new and sustained relationships to accomplish stated goals. The smallest instance would be marriage, and the largest would be to overthrow an old and create a new society. A setting need not be tied to a particular, bounded space. The development of any network can be viewed as the creation of a setting, and therefore the problems of leadership have to be seen in terms of the early context of development." This quote is from *The Challenge of the Resource Exchange Network*, p. 143 (see note 20).

22. Elizabeth Lorentz told us this story during an interview at The Networking Institute, West Newton, Massachusetts, December 13, 1993.

23. This description of Mrs. Dewar's mind is from *The Challenge of the Resource Exchange Network*, p. 145 (see note 20).

24. For their first thinking on the coordinator role, see *Human Services and Resource Networks: Rationale, Possibilities, and Public Policy*, by

Seymour B. Sarason, Charles F. Carroll, Kenneth Maton, Saul Cohen, and Elizabeth Lorentz (San Francisco: Jossey-Bass, 1977; Cambridge, MA: Brookline Books, 1988), p. xvii.

25. From this point on, all quotes in this chapter, unless otherwise noted, are from "Draft—The Coordinator Role in Networking: J.-J. New Book Chapter," by Elizabeth Lorentz, March, 1994.

26. The quote on the coordinator's job as a matchmaker is from *The Challenge of the Resource Exchange Network*, p. 145 (see note 20).

27. Because of its decentralized nature, no one knows the precise size of the Internet. One of the pioneers in tracking Internet growth is John Quarterman at Matrix Index and Directory Services (MIDS), who calls it "the "matrix." This quote is from his article "How Big Is the Matrix?" *Matrix News*, Vol. 2, No. 2, Index (Matrix and Directory, Austin, TX, 1992). Quarterman's Internet address is jsq@tic.com.

Chapter 8

1. This quote from historian Frederic Lane, which we found in *Making Democracy Work: Civic Traditions in Modern Italy*, by Robert D. Putnam (Princeton, NJ: Princeton University Press, 1993), p. 124, originally appeared in *Venice and History*, by Frederic C. Lane (Baltimore: Johns Hopkins University Press, 1966), p. 535. We are indebted to Putnam for much of the information on which this section is based.

2. This quote from *Making Democracy Work* (see note 1), p. 129, is originally from *Before the Industrial Revolution: European Society and Economy, 1000–1700*, 2nd ed., by Carlo M. Cippola (London: Methuen, 1980), pp. 198–199.

3. The rise of small business networks was the "hot news" that many business writers and reviewers picked out of *The TeamNet Factor*.

4. Stuart Rosenfeld is the founder and executive director of Regional Technology Strategies, P.O. Box 9005, Chapel Hill, NC 27515; telephone: 919-933-6699.

5. *Making Democracy Work* (see note 1) describes in detail the work of Putnam and his two Italian colleagues and many collaborators in Italy.

6. There was enormous disparity in social services between the north and the south. For example, Emilia-Romagna had one child-care center per 400 children; Campania, in the south, had 300 percent fewer, one per 12,560 children.

7. For the detailed analysis of Emilia-Romagna's "good government," reporting the study's composite index of institutional performance, see *Making Democracy Work*, p. 76 (see note 1).

8. All three maps are from *Making Democracy Work* (see note 1). The first, "Institutional Performance in Italian Regions," is map figure 4.1, p. 84. Copyright © 1993 by Princeton University Press. Reproduced by permission of Princeton University Press.

9. The second map, "Republican and Autocratic Traditions," is map figure 4.4, p. 97. Copyright © 1993 by Princeton University Press. Reproduced by permission of Princeton University Press.

10. The third map, "Civic Community in Italian Regions," is map figure 5.1, p. 134. Copyright © 1993 by Princeton University Press. Reproduced by permission of Princeton University Press.

11. The quote on civil communities is from *Making Democracy Work*, p. 88 (see note 1).

12. The quote on the dense "concentration of overlapping networks" is from *Making Democracy Work*, p. 115 (see note 1).

13. Social capital has been a research topic and a concept under development for more than a decade, especially in sociology. See Ronald S. Burt, *Structural Holes: The Social Structure of Competition* (Cambridge, MA: Harvard University Press, 1992), for an excellent treatment. We use Putnam's formulation here.

14. The quote on reciprocity is from *Making Democracy Work*, p. 139 (see note 1).

15. This quote was taken from *The Trust Factor*, by John O. Whitney (New York: McGraw-Hill, 1994), p. 11, which contains an excellent discussion of trust.

16. For a superb three-part series on problems in the fishing industry, see "Troubled Waters: Fishing in Crisis," by Colin Nickerson, whose first article, "Stripping the Sea's Life," *The Boston Sunday Globe*, April 17, 1994, jumped from p. 1 to p. 24, where it had the headline "Greed, Mismanagement Ravage Fisheries."

17. The observation that cooperation becomes increasingly rational and practical is from *The Evolution of Cooperation*, by Robert Axelrod (New York: Basic Books, 1984).

18. For an excellent treatment of systems dynamics, see *The Fifth Discipline: The Art & Science of the Learning Organization*, by Peter Senge (New York: Doubleday, 1990).

19. The quote on defection is from Robert Sugden, as quoted in *Making Democracy Work*, p. 178 (see note 1).

20. Among the first to report on the Emilia-Romagna "miracle" were Michael J. Piore and Charles F. Sabel in their book *The Second Industrial Divide: Possibilities for Prosperity* (New York: Basic Books, 1994).

21. For a superb treatment of this topic, see *Regional Advantage: Culture and Competition in Silicon Valley and Route 128*, by AnnaLee Saxenian (Cambridge, MA: Harvard University Press, 1994).

22. These points are made in Saxenian's article, "Silicon Valley Versus Route 128," *Inc.*, February 1994, p. 25.

23. The quote about DEC is also from Saxenian's *Inc.* article, p. 26.

24. On p. 50 of *Regional Advantage* (see note 21), Saxenian quotes the Harvard Business School case study of Hewlett-Packard.

25. The quote about Ken Olsen's management model is from *Regional Advantage*, p. 74 (see note 21).

26. The quote about DEC's power structure is from *Regional Advantage*, p. 76 (see note 21).

27. We are grateful to Joe Szocik of the Attleboro Area Center for Training (96 Pine Street, Attleboro, MA 02703; telephone: 508-222-0096) for the excellent memos he sent us emphasizing the challenges of economic disparities.

28. We thank David Williams of High Point, North Carolina, for sending us the article "A Timely Warning to the Developed World" by Michael Valpy, *The Globe and Mail*, December 17, 1993, p. A2, from which the quote on social capital was taken.

29. Ashby's seminal article "Variety, Constraint, and the Law of Requisite Variety," drawn from his book, *An Introduction to Cybernetics* (London: Chapman and Hall, 1956), appears in *Modern Systems Research for the Behavioral Scientist: A Sourcebook*, edited by Walter Buckley (Chicago: Aldine, 1968), p. 129.

30. For the basis of this important concept, see "The Strength of Weak Ties," by Mark S. Granovetter, *American Journal of Sociology*, Vol. 78, No. 6, pp. 1360–1380.

31. See *Structural Holes* (see note 13) for a similar idea that helps to maximize the efficiency and effectiveness of networks.

Chapter 9

1. The description of AT&T Universal Card Services' learning partnerships is from a conversation with Mike Plummer, June 24, 1994.

2. In our first book, *Networking: The First Report and Directory*, published by Doubleday in April 1982, we included a list of emerging trends. John Naisbitt, then of the polling firm Yankelovich, Skelly, and White, had monitored local newspapers to spot emerging trends, and his published list showed up in a computer conference we were part of on the Electronic Information Exchange System. Number one on his list was "FROM Industrial Society TO Information Society." We were astonished when, in September of that same year, we received an autographed advance copy of *Megatrends: Ten New Directions Transforming Our Lives* (New York: Warner Books, 1982) with a note from Naisbitt, who was on his way to achieving a very big best-seller. The revised and sharpened set now included an eighth megatrend—"FROM Hierarchies TO Networking"—and an extensive quote from an earlier article of ours, which had appeared in *New Age*. See *Megatrends*, p. 193, for the quote.

3. For more on reengineering, see *Reengineering the Corporation: A Manifesto for Business Revolution*, by Michael Hammer and James Champy (New York: HarperBusiness, 1993).

4. The definition of a team is from *The Wisdom of Teams: Creating the High-Performance Organization*, by Jon R. Katzenbach and Douglas K. Smith (Boston: Harvard Business School Press, 1993), p. 45.

5. For the classic work on the learning organization, see *The Fifth Discipline: The Art & Practice of The Learning Organization*, by Peter M. Senge (New York: Doubleday/Currency, 1990), where the quote appears on p. 3; see also *The Fifth Discipline Fieldbook*, by Peter M. Senge, Charlotte Roberts, Richard B. Ross, Bryan J. Smith, and Art Kleiner (New York: Doubleday/Currency, 1994).

6. Hierarchies may be logically considered a special case of networks.

7. Deming used somewhat different wording for these points at various times. The group here is drawn mainly from a December, 1989 set. See *The Team Handbook: How to Use Teams to Improve Quality*, by Peter R. Scholtes et al. (Madison, WI: Joiner Associates, Inc., 1992), pp. 2–24.

8. Population is only one exponential growth factor. See the "hinge of history" graphic in chapter 6, p. 142 of this book, for others.

9. For more on the burgeoning vision "business," see "Visioning' Missions Becomes Its Own Mission," by Gilbert Fuchsberg, *The Wall Street Journal*, January 7, 1994, p. B1.

10. One excellent article on separatism, from which this quote was taken, is "Global Paradox; Growth of Trade Binds Nations, But It Also Can Spur Separatism; Dissident Groups Worry Less About the Economic Cost of Going Their Own Way; A World of 500 Countries?" by Bob Davis, *The Wall Street Journal*, June 20, 1994, p. A1.

11. For an early visionary piece about networking (written in 1987), see "Anything, Anytime, Anywhere: The Future of Networking," by William R. Johnson, Jr., in *Technology 2001: The Future of Computing and Communications*, Derek Leebaert, ed. (Cambridge, MA: MIT Press, 1991), pp. 149–175.

12. The quote on information sharing is from Levi Strauss's CEO, Robert Haas in "The New Post-Heroic Leadership," by John Huey, *Fortune*, February 21, 1994, p. 48.

13. See "The Technology Payoff: A Sweeping Reorganization of Work Itself Is Boosting Productivity," Special Report by Howard Gleckman et al., *Business Week*, June 14, 1993, pp. 57–68.

14. "High-tech/high-touch" is John Naisbitt's term from *Megatrends*, (see note 2), p. 1.

15. The quote on business's $1 trillion investment in information technology is from the cover of *Business Week* (see note 13).

16. For more on building a culture where "we're all bosses," see *The New Partnership: Profit by Bringing Out the Best in Your People, Customers, & Yourself*, by Tom Melohn (Essex Junction, VT: Oliver Wight/Omneo, 1994), p. 45.

17. For an excellent discussion of top-level teams, see "Teams at the Top," by Marc Hequet, *Training*, April, 1994, p. 9, from which this quote is taken.

18. The quote on power sharing is from the *Fortune* cover story (see note 12), pp. 42–56.

19. For more on W. L. Gore & Associates, see our third book, *The TeamNet Factor* (Essex Junction, VT: Oliver Wight, 1993), pp. 80–84.

20. Many people invented the term "netweaver": Pat Wagner and Leif Smith of Denver, Colorado's, Office for Open Network; Peter+Trudy

Johnson-Lenz of Lake Oswego, Oregon, inventors of the term "groupware," meaning computer software that enhances the ability of a group to work together; and Frank Burns and Lisa Kimball of MetaSystems Design Group in Arlington, VA. Most recently, we heard the term again from Carlos Nagel of the International Sonora Desert Alliance, who writes, "I now think of myself as a net*weaver* as much as a net*worker*." The story of how Nagel used networking to save the Michoacan sea turtles appears in *The Networking Book* (London: Viking Penguin, 1986), our second book, pp. 116–118.

21. For a superb treatment of the use of networks, see *The New Organization: Growing the Culture of Organizational Networking*, by Colin Hastings (London: McGraw-Hill, 1993), p. 162.

22. The quote on the absence of teams at the top is from the *Training* article (see note 17), p. 8.

23. For more on the structure of Asea Brown Boveri, see *The TeamNet Factor*, pp. 61–67 (see note 19).

24. Koestler wrote such powerful literary classics as *Darkness at Noon* (London: Jonathan Cape, 1940); a history of science with popular appeal, *The Sleepwalkers* (New York: Macmillan, 1959); and cross-disciplinary scientific works with a universal human core, such as *The Act of Creation* (New York: Macmillan, 1964) and *The Ghost in the Machine* (London: Hutchinson & Co., 1967), where he introduced the concept of the holon.

25. For more on Alexander's systems view of design, see *A Pattern Language* (see chapter 7, this book, note 11).

26. For more on systems and networks, see "Transforming Bureaucracies and Systems," the Reference Section of *The TeamNet Factor*, pp. 359–382 (see note 19).

27. The Santa Fe Institute, 1120 Canyon Road, Santa Fe, NM 87501, is a good example of practical cross-boundary science growing in the 1990s, where a network of associates and residencies, established by, among others, the conceptual father of quarks, Murray Gel-Mann, studies and models complexity.

28. Holonomy means "the systematized knowledge of holons." See *Holonomy: A Human Systems Theory*, by Jeffrey S. Stamps, with a foreword by systems pioneer Kenneth Boulding (Seaside, CA: Intersystems Publications, 1980), p. 7.

29. For more on applying terms of negative and positive feedback in general systems theory, see *The Fifth Discipline*, pp. 79–92 (see note 5).
30. The quote on rethinking the office "from the ground up" is from "In New Jersey, I.B.M. Cuts Space, Frills and Private Desks," by Kirk Johnson, *The New York Times*, March 14, 1994, p. B1.
31. The "personal harbor" and "commons" sketch appears here courtesy of Steelcase, Inc. The drawing first appeared in "Field Research and Knowledge Work Process," by Paul Cornell and Pam Brenner, both of Steelcase's Research and Business Development Group, International Facilities Management Association 93 Conference Proceedings, October, 1993.
32. For more on the "quality without a name," see *The Timeless Way of Building* (chapter 7, this book, note 11).

INDEX

ABOUT THE AUTHORS

Jessica Lipnack and Jeffrey Stamps, Ph.D., are the principals of The Networking Institute, Inc., (TNI) a consulting firm in West Newton, Massachusetts. Founded by them in 1982, TNI *helps people work together better across boundaries*, including geographic, organizational, corporate, industrial, and governmental boundaries. TNI offers consulting services, public and in-house workshops and seminars, and provides *TeamNet Tools*, software for networks of teams.

Frequent keynoters at conferences, Jessica and Jeff have spoken and consulted for a wide variety of organizations throughout the United States, as well as in Canada, Europe, Japan, and Australia. This is their fourth book on networking. Previous books include *The TeamNet Factor: Bringing the Power of Boundary Crossing into the Heart of Your Business* (Oliver Wight, 1993); *The Networking Book: People Connecting with People* (Viking Penguin, 1986), foreword by R. Buckminster Fuller; and *Networking: The First Report and Directory* (Doubleday, 1982). Jeff is also author of *Holonomy: A Human Systems Theory* (Intersystems, 1980), which was his doctoral dissertation on general systems theory that includes a foreword by Kenneth Boulding.

Clients have included AT&T Universal Card Services, British Petroleum Exploration, CSC Index, Digital Equipment Corporation (1985–1992), Hyatt Hotels, KPMG Peat Marwick, Presbyterian Church (U.S.A.), Shell Offshore, Inc., Steelcase, Inc., the United Nations, and Vice President Gore's National Performance Review.

Jessica and Jeff have been working together since 1968 when they met at Oxford University. Married in 1972, they are parents of two daughters, Miranda and Eliza, and reside in West Newton, Massachusetts.

We encourage you to call, fax, e-mail, and send materials to:

The Networking Institute, Inc.
Drawer AN
505 Waltham Street
West Newton, MA 02165 USA

Telephone: 1-617-965-3340
Fax: 1-617-965-2341
E-mail: info@netage·com